TeXt FoR SeotLaNd

Building Excellence in Language

S1

Colin Eckford
Caroline Harper
Gary Smith

www.heinemann.co.uk

✓ Free online support
✓ Useful weblinks
✓ 24 hour online ordering

01865 888118

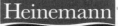

Contents

Contents

1 A life's story

Experiences and outcomes

In this unit you will:

Reading

- decide how to use information from different sources
- use reading strategies to get information from texts
- make notes of key points to use later in writing.

Writing

- organise texts to make their meaning clear
- start paragraphs using key sentences to show what the paragraph has in it; sequence correctly
- use tense consistently so that meaning is clear
- understand and use the terms 'noun', 'verb' and 'contractions'.

Punctuation and spelling

- use punctuation between sentences and clauses to make meaning clear; revise capital letters and full stops.

By the end of this unit you will:

- get information from sources and make notes (Reading Activity: Reading for information)
- write a biography (Writing Activity: Functional writing).

1 Biography and autobiography

You are learning:

● to understand the terms 'biography' and 'autobiography'.

An autobiography is the story of someone's life written by that person. A biography is the story of someone's life written by someone else. When we read autobiographies and biographies we learn about a person's life. We may be inspired by their achievements, or we may just learn more about their everyday lives.

Activity 1

Look at the front covers of these biographies and autobiographies.

Using a table like the one below, decide which are autobiographies and which are biographies. Make sure you can justify your choices.

	Biography (✓)	Autobiography (✓)	What are your reasons?
1			
2			

Activity 2

A blurb informs people about a book's contents in order to encourage them to buy it.

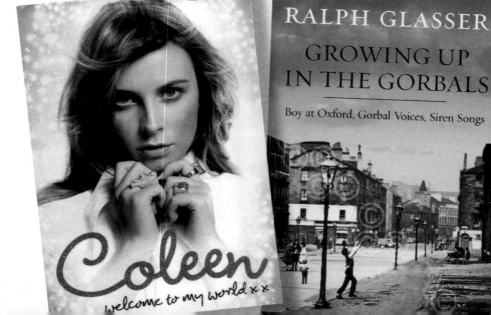

1 Read the blurbs from the two autobiographies below and look at their front covers on page 6. These two books would probably appeal to different groups of people (or 'audiences'). For each blurb, and the cover that goes with it, say whether you think the book would be enjoyed most by:

a males, females or everybody.

b people your age, people older than you or everybody.

Explain why you think this.

Blurb A

Her story is a Cinderella Fairytale of an ordinary Liverpudlian school girl who was transformed into a style icon and cover girl, sought after by fashion and lifestyle magazines the world over.

Welcome to my world is Coleen's chance to reflect on this amazing journey and share her love of fashion with her fans. From puffa jackets to Prada bags, Coleen reveals the secrets behind her famous wardrobe, her style, her guide to shopping, her dos and don'ts, her beauty regimes and her body workouts. It's also the story of a young girl who has managed to keep true to her working-class roots whilst being catapulted into a world beyond her wildest dreams.

From *Welcome to my world* by Coleen McLoughlin

Blurb B

Ralph Glasser's *Gorbals Trilogy* is an extraordinary account of a remarkable life. In *Growing up in the Gorbals,* Glasser describes his childhood and adolescence in the impoverished slums of the Glasgow tenements in the 1920s and the hardships and heartaches that went with it. At 14 he left school to become a barber's soap boy but he soon started the night classes that would eventually lead him to a scholarship to Oxford. In *Gorbals Boy at Oxford* he describes his new life, the incredible characters he met and the arrogance of Oxford academic life, and in *Gorbals Voices, Siren Songs*, Ralph Glasser's brilliant trilogy concludes in the wayward world of post-war London.

From *Growing up in the Gorbals* by Ralph Glasser

2 Some public figures have a 'ghost writer', a professional writer who either improves their autobiography or writes the vast majority of it for them. Which of the texts above do you think is more likely to have had a ghost writer and why?

Knowledge about language: Nouns and verbs

Nouns are naming words. Nouns usually have 'a', 'an' or 'the' in front of them.

Verbs are doing words and tell us what a person or thing does.

1 Look again at Blurb A. List the nouns in the last sentence, which begins 'It's also the story ...'

2 Look at Blurb B. List the verbs in the third sentence 'At 14 he left school ...'

2 Reading and researching

You are learning:
- to find the information you need.

Skimming and scanning are important reading skills.

Skimming helps you read quickly to get the overall gist of a text to decide whether it contains the information you need.

Scanning is a way of looking for specific information in a text. You do not need to read every word. You can use headings and titles to help you locate your information. This is a reading skill you use when you look up words in a dictionary, or search for telephone numbers in a directory.

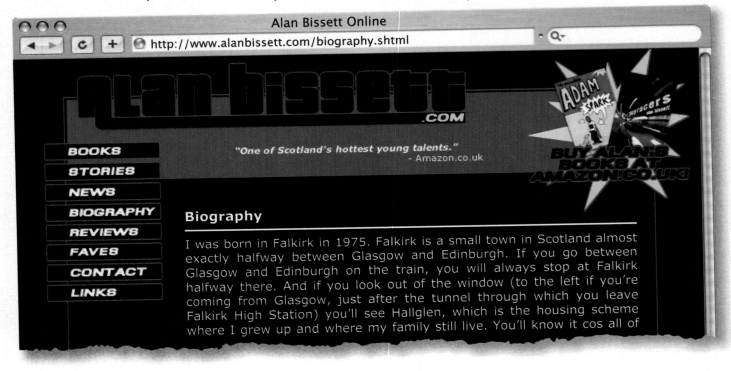

Activity 1

1 Read the research topics in the table below. Skim page 9, which is taken from the poet Alan Bissett's personal website. Decide how useful the web page would be if you were researching the topics in the table below. Try to do this in two minutes. 🕐 **2 minutes**

Research topic	Useful? Yes (✓) No (X)
a Facts about Bissett's professional achievements	
b Interviews with Bissett	
c Information about what Bissett is currently doing	
d Blurbs from Bissett's novels for teenagers	
e Information about Bissett's childhood	
f Pictures of Bissett and details about how to contact him	

Alan Bissett Online

http://www.alanbissett.com/biography.shtml

ALAN BISSETT .COM

BOOKS
STORIES
NEWS
BIOGRAPHY
REVIEWS
FAVES
CONTACT
LINKS

"One of Scotland's hottest young talents."
- Amazon.co.uk

BUY ALAN'S BOOKS AT AMAZON.CO.UK!

Biography

I was born in Falkirk in 1975. Falkirk is a small town in Scotland almost exactly halfway between Glasgow and Edinburgh. If you go between Glasgow and Edinburgh on the train, you will always stop at Falkirk halfway there. And if you look out of the window (to the left if you're coming from Glasgow, just after the tunnel through which you leave Falkirk High Station) you'll see Hallglen, which is the housing scheme where I grew up and where my family still live. You'll know it cos all of the buildings are white. Or at least they used to be. Now they're a kind of dull grey colour.

I went to Hallglen Primary School, which I loved, and Falkirk High School, which I didn't enjoy very much, mainly cos I was one of those depressed teenagers that we keep reading about these days. Then I went to Stirling University and got a First in English and Education, which surprised everyone, not least me. After a spell teaching English in secondary schools, I got tired of not being a student and went back to study for a PhD.

I didn't get a PhD. But I did get two books published. And those books were *Boyracers* (which I done wrote) and *Damage Land* (which I done edited). During that time I was also shortlisted for the now-defunct but then-prestigious Macallan/Scotland on Sunday Short-story Competition, but didn't win it, which is a shame, as seven grand always comes in handy. Especially when you're a student. I was long- or short-listed for this award every year for four years, without ever winning it. I was hoping they were just going to give it to me out of sympathy one year.

Hey ho. I then lectured in Creative Writing at the Bretton Hall campus of the University of Leeds for about three years, where I wrote my second novel, *The Incredible Adam Spark*. Now I teach on the MPhil in Creative Writing at the University of Glasgow, which has produced almost every new writer in Scotland and their aunty. Unfortunately, I can't take credit for any of them, as they had all graduated before I arrived.

I live in Glasgow, but I visit Falkirk and Leeds a lot. I write stuff. I have a brother, a sister, a mum and a dad. I have two wee nephews. They are ace. And that's it really. Most writers have deeply boring lives. Unless you're George Orwell, and get shot fighting in a war or sleep on the streets for research and stuff. And I don't fancy that much, sorry.

I also like cherry-coke and peach schnapps.

2 Look again at page 9. Where on this web page would you click to find information on the following research topics? Use a table like the one below. Try to do this in two minutes.

🕐 2 minutes

Research topic	What I would click on
Information on Bissett's novels	Books
Information on Bissett's favourite films	
People and personal contacts that are part of Bissett's life	
Examples and cuttings of media articles on the writer	

Activity 2

1 The picture below shows the part of Scotland known as the Central Belt where Falkirk, Hallglen, Edinburgh and Glasgow are found. Scan Bissett's web page and decide which number corresponds to which town or city.

2 Bissett says: 'I live in Glasgow, but I visit Falkirk and Leeds a lot.' Scan his website and explain why he might want to visit:
   a Falkirk
   b Leeds.

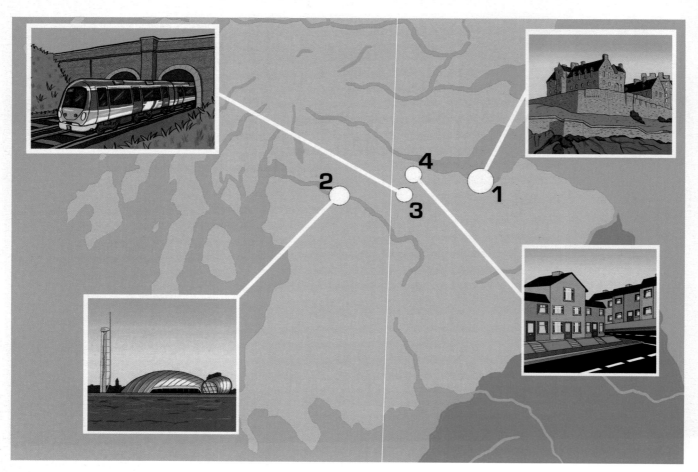

Self-evaluation

Look at the skills you have been practising on pages 8–10. How well are you doing? Pick the traffic light that shows how confident you feel in each area.

- I understand the difference between skimming and scanning.
- I can use skimming skills to decide whether a text might be relevant for what I need.
- I can use scanning skills to find and select specific information.
- I can identify examples in the text that support my opinions.

not confident

quite confident

very confident

Knowledge about language: Capital letters and full stops

Read the biographical details below about Hugh MacDiarmid, who used Scots as a written language again, although for centuries it had been only a spoken language. Use what you have learned about full stops and capital letters to rewrite the passage correcting the errors.

Remember
- Every sentence must begin with a capital letter.
- Proper nouns must begin with a capital letter.
- Use a full stop to end any sentence that is not a question or an exclamation.

Hugh MacDiarmid was born in 1872 in langholm in dumfriesshire. He became a journalist but, during world War I he joined the royal Army medical Corps and served all over europe

He was a strong Scottish nationalist and believed that Scots could only truly express themselves in the scots language he began to recreate a written Scots language with words used in different parts of the country. Soon he was publishing his poetry, written in Scots his most famous collection was *A Drunk Man Looks at the Thistle* in 1926.

By the 1950s, a number of poets, such as Robert garioch, william Soutar and Sidney goodsir smith were using the Scots language to write modern poetry.

More recently, some writers have chosen to use scots for writing novels they include James kelman from glasgow, Irvine welsh from edinburgh, and alan bissett from falkirk.

3 Note-taking

Making notes can help you to make sense of a text. It can also improve your memory of what you have read. It helps you to write the key learning points in your own words, without copying out a text in full.

Activity 1

John Logie Baird was the inventor of television.

1   Read the biographical information about the childhood of John Logie Baird.

John Logie Baird

'Very slow', 'timid' and 'by no means a quick learner'

As a boy:

John Logie Baird was born on 14 August 1888, the fourth child of Jessie and the Reverend John Baird. His family lived in a large house called 'The Lodge' in Helensburgh, a coastal town which lies 25 miles north-west of Glasgow. By the turn of the twentieth century, this house had seen the development of a telephone exchange, had been supplied with electric lighting and had been the site of an early flight experiment, all of which were the work of the imaginative youngest child.

A telephone exchange was quite an achievement for a young schoolboy. Other children played with tin cans and pieces of string, but John Baird had tried this method and was dissatisfied. Instead, he made an electric exchange and connected his home to those of four of his friends. Unfortunately this telephone service was not in use for very long, as one of its low hanging wires caused the driver of a hansom cab to have an accident. This driver's protests soon led to the removal of the telephone wires from their various positions around the neighbourhood. Never one to waste resources, the boy then used the wires from his telephone exchange to set up a lighting system for The Lodge. Run by a petrol-powered generator in the back garden, this activity made his parents' home the first in Helensburgh to have electric lighting.

John Logie Baird was also conducting experiments in other areas of research. The first year of the twentieth century saw the young inventor standing on the roof of his parents' house with a home-made glider. This experiment took place on a flat section of the roof of The Lodge, and had a rather strong impact on the rest of Baird's life. The glider was constructed with the assistance of his friend Godfrey Harris, but may not have been as well designed or constructed as some of his later machinery. Baird describes this incident in his autobiography *Sermons, Soap and Television*:

'I had no intention of flying, but before I had time to give more than one shriek of alarm, Godfrey gave the machine one terrific push, and I was launched shrieking into the air. I had a few very nauseating seconds while the machine rocked wildly and then broke in half and deposited me with a terrific bump on the lawn.'

A healthy social life and an inventive nature seemed to be at variance with Baird's school career. The twelve-year-old boy is described in his school report as 'very slow,' 'timid' and 'by no means a quick learner.' Nevertheless, Baird was not discouraged by his academic record, and in 1906 entered a diploma course in electrical engineering at the Glasgow and West of Scotland Technical College.

From *Eye of the World: John Logie Baird and Television (Part 1)*, by Adrian R Hills

2 Write down five **key words** that sum up Baird's childhood.

3 Now close this book and expand your key words by writing notes from memory.

4 Summarise what you have learned about Baird's childhood.

Activity 2

The text on page 12 about John Logie Baird is organised chronologically, which means that events are described in the order in which they occurred. Use a timeline like the one illustrated opposite to summarise the key points in Baird's life that predicted his future achievements.

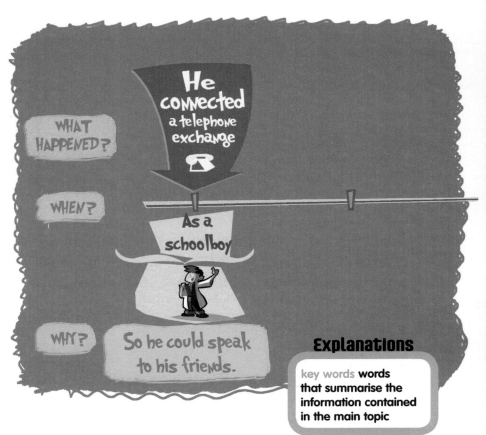

Explanations

key words **words that summarise the information contained in the main topic**

Knowledge about language: **Sequencing**

The points below summarise key points about John Logie Baird's adult life. Put them into the correct order. Write down the word or words that helped you correctly place each section in the sequence.

① In 1925 Baird succeeded in showing a dummy's head on television.

② During World War I it is thought that Baird was trying to develop secret signalling for the British Army.

③ After television, Baird went on to develop television for cinemas, and investigate secret signalling and radar technology.

④ Four months later he demonstrated his television to the Royal Institute.

⑤ World War I broke out before Baird completed his degree and he was not accepted into the army. He continued his investigations, including work on television.

4 Fact and opinion

You are learning:
● to distinguish between fact and opinion.

A fact is something that is true. An opinion is somebody's point of view.

Activity 1

1   Read these two texts about Shaun Ellis. Text A gives information about his life. Text B is a TV channel's introduction to a programme before it is broadcast.

Text A

Biography

Shaun Ellis is a man in wolf's clothing, living wild with them and talking their language ... literally. For a raw-meat-eating 'wild animal' used to roaming his environment by night and marking his territory wherever he pleases, Shaun Ellis comes across as a surprisingly civilised individual. Well-spoken, intelligent and passionate, it's only the excessively shaggy beard and straggly hair that give him away as one of the leading members of a pack of wolves.

Three years ago, the 42-year-old decided the only way to really get to know his beloved wolves was to become one of them. He entered an enclosure at a wildlife park in North Devon, along with three abandoned new-born cubs, and became the alpha male of the group, raising the small family as his own. For the first 18 months, he was in the enclosure 24/7 and even now spends most of his time, and almost all of his evenings, huddled up alongside his wolf family.

He has learned to eat raw meat straight off the carcass of a dead animal, communicate with them by howling, and is covered in scratches and wounds from his playful wrestles and fights with his 'brothers'.

But as unusual a lifestyle as this sounds, this is not some mid-life crisis, breakdown or attempt to turn his back on society. Shaun's adventure has been a long-standing scientific study into the lifestyle of his favourite animal and has so far produced some incredible results.

Eventually, he hopes to put his findings to good use and boost the campaign to reintroduce wild wolves to areas such as the Highlands, where they haven't been seen living free for hundreds of years.

He feels that working with animals and trying to understand how they live is what he was put on this planet to do, and he has travelled the world to get closer to nature.

Text B

Wolf Man

Explore the crazy world of wolf-man and researcher Shaun Ellis, who has lived among wolves to research the way they live. In our unmissable documentary, *Wolf Man*, watch the extraordinary behaviour of this man, who has left his everyday life to live among beasts as he becomes leader of the pack, learns their ways and acts like them. An opportunity to have an amazing insight into his unique life and these fascinating animals!

2 Text A contains writing to inform . It is a recount text and contains facts to inform the reader. The table below gives the features of a recount text. Find an example of each feature in Text A, then copy and complete the table.

Feature of recount text	Example
Events written in time order (chronological order)	
Linking words related to time (e.g. *later, twenty years on*)	
Dialogue or reported speech to reveal information about the character	
Specific dates, times, people and places	
Answers to the questions *when, where, who, what, why*	

3 Text B contains writing to persuade. The writer of this text chooses words to persuade people to watch the programme.
  a List five words or expressions about Shaun Ellis in Text B which are opinions rather than facts.
  b Choose three from your list. For each one, explain why these words or expressions might persuade people to watch the programme.

4 Which of the two texts would be more useful and reliable if you were researching the life of Shaun Ellis? Give reasons for your answer.

Self-evaluation

A key skill in reading and research is being able to use evidence from texts to back up your views.

How confident were you in completing questions 2 and 3 above? Look again at the quotations you picked. Are they effective evidence for the questions you were asked? You might like to discuss your choices with a partner and compare your selections.

Choose the traffic light that shows how confident you feel in selecting evidence.

not confident

quite confident

very confident

5 Gathering evidence

You are learning:
● to decide where you might find relevant information and then select what you need.

Information is now available in far more ranges and formats than in the past: film, radio, TV, the Internet, ICT resources, books, newspapers and magazines. It is important to be able to know where to find what you need, select what is useful and then organise it.

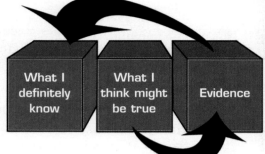

Activity 1

You are going to complete a research task to understand more about autism. Talk with a partner or group about anything you already know about autism. Use a diagram like the one opposite to summarise what you **know** about the condition, what you **think** you know about it, and what you want to **find out** about it.

Activity 2

Below are links from the National Autistic Society website. Which of the linked pages would be most useful for finding out facts about autism? Give reasons for your choice.

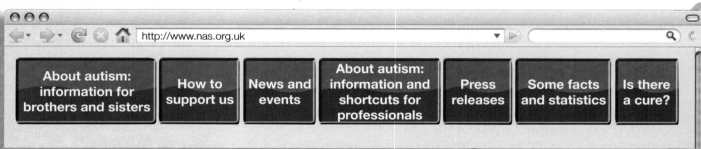

Activity 3

The following extract describes the writer's experience of living with a sibling who is autistic. Read the extract, then create a diagram along the lines of the one in Activity 1, using the information you have read about autism.

Communication

Okay, let's start with number one, **difficulty with communication**. Some people with autism do not speak, or some people have difficulty speaking. For those who do not speak, they may use pictures, written words or even something called sign language (hand or arm movements) to tell people what they need or how they are feeling.

My brother sometimes takes my hand or shows me what he wants instead of speaking because he finds this easier to do. My brother can speak but sometimes it takes him a long time to say something back to me. If I say lots of words at once, he can become very confused, so I must remember to keep things simple and sometimes say things slowly.

My brother also has problems working out when someone is joking or teasing him. To help him understand jokes, I sometimes have to say that I was joking.

We understand how people are feeling by looking at their faces. My brother and people with autism find it very hard to understand faces. For example, my brother doesn't seem to know when I'm angry or upset.

Sometimes he copies or even laughs at me. He doesn't mean this to be horrible, he just doesn't know what to do when I am feeling like this. Sometimes he thinks I'm just pulling a funny face, which is why he laughs at me, but a lot of the time he doesn't realise that he should help me or leave me alone.

Knowledge about language: The past tense

Autobiographies and biographies are usually written in the past tense as they describe events that have already happened. The autobiographical passage below taken from an article called 'B is for Bestseller' is by the author Mark Haddon, who also wrote a well-known book about a boy with Asperger's Syndrome called *The Curious Incident of the Dog in the Night-Time*.

1   Find one sentence that is written in the past tense. Explain why the writer uses the past tense at that point.

2   Find one sentence that is written in the present tense. Explain why the writer uses the present tense at this point.

Three years ago, I wrote *The Curious Incident of the Dog in the Night-Time*, a novel set in Swindon about a teenage boy with Asperger's syndrome who discovers a murdered poodle on a neighbour's lawn. It was published in two identical editions with different covers, one for adults and one for teenagers. To my continuing amazement, it seems to have spread round the world like some particularly infectious rash.

6 Preparing an essay

You are learning:
- to sequence text logically and use topic sentences.

Half the success of an essay is in the structure and development. Topic sentences give clarity and purpose to your essay.

Activity 1

You are going to write about the Scottish tennis star Andy Murray for a magazine aimed at British teenagers. In order to research your article, you have three texts to use: a profile from the British Tennis website (Text A), an interview with the sportsman himself (Text B), and a newspaper article about him describing some of his achievements in his first two years after turning professional (Text C).

1 Read Texts A, B and C.

Text A

File   Edit   View   Favorites   Tools   Help

Address http://www.lta.org.uk

Player profile

Andy Murray

Date of birth: 15.5.87

Birthplace: Dunblane, Scotland

Lives in: Dunblane, Scotland

Country: Scotland

Club: Bridge of Allan Sports Club

Trains at: National Tennis Centre, Roehampton, London

Coach: Miles MacLagan

Former coaches: Leon Smith, Mark Petchey, Pato Alvares, Brad Gilbert

Height: 6ft 2"

Plays: Right-handed, two-handed backhand

Nickname: Muzcat

Fitness trainer: Jezz Green/Matt Little

Favourite surface: Hard

Introduction to tennis: At Dunblane Sports Club with his mother

Age turned pro: 17

Age started playing: 3

Injury history: Knee injury from Dec 03–May 04. Right wrist, June 06.

Career-high singles world ranking: No. 8 (June 07)

2007 highlights: Broke into ATP singles world top 10 at No.10 for the first time on 16.4.07
Reached semi-finals of the Miami Masters Series.
Reached the semi-finals of the Pacific Life Open Masters Series
Won his second ATP singles title, the SAP Open, in San Jose

Junior career highlights

Winner US Open Boys' Singles Championships 2004

Doubles semi-finalist with brother Jamie at US Open Juniors

Winner of the 12-and-under Orange Bowl World Championships, Florida

Text B

File Edit View Favorites Tools Help

Address | http://www.childrenfirstforhealth.co.uk

Andy Murray – Tennis player

Scotland's smash-hit tennis star Andy Murray talks to Camilla Francis about the green grass of Wimbledon, his favourite food and how he keeps fit.

You were aged three when you started playing tennis. Did you take to it from the word 'go'?

No, my mum had to throw lots and lots of balls to me until I started to connect racket and ball! Then I got a swingball for my garden and I loved that. I could hit it as hard as I wanted and it didn't break anything, and the ball always came back!

Did tennis take over your life as a child and how much training did you have to put in?

No, I played football and golf too. When I was 12 or 13 I started to train more – probably about 1.5 hours a day.

Did your parents encourage you to play?

Yes, my mum is a tennis coach and my dad would hit balls about, but I could beat him when I was about six!

Apart from tennis what else do you do to keep fit?

I play golf, go to the gym and sometimes play football – but not as much as I would like to.

Do you pay special attention to your diet? Are there things you avoid or super-foods that you eat lots of?

I eat a lot of pasta when I am competing. I like salad and steak, and sometimes I treat myself to fries! But I usually try to avoid fatty foods. I love Häagen-Dazs ice cream and fresh fruit. I don't drink or smoke.

How much do you think your health affects your game?

I play my best when I feel fresh. I am still growing so I still get quite tired easily. I like to sleep a lot!

Do you feel your lifestyle varies a lot to other young people your age?

It has to be a bit different because I am travelling a lot but I still try to go out with friends when I get the chance.

Do you worry about injury and ill health?

No, I don't worry about it until it happens. If I look after my body I would hope to avoid ill health and injury – but sometimes you can't control these things.

How do you prepare for a game?

Early to bed, a good breakfast – fresh fruit, bagel and cream cheese, apple and raspberry juice. I practise for half an hour, then do a physical warm-up for about 20 minutes before the match in the locker room. I go over my tactics with my coach. I listen to my iPod… I'm ready to go then!

Text C

Stirling Observer, 7 December 2005

ANDY JOINS SPORT ELITE

TENNIS prodigy Andrew Murray will be one of the favourites to pick up this year's BBC Sports Personality of the Year on Sunday.

The Dunblane teenager has had a remarkable year, coming from nowhere to reach a top-70 position in the world rankings.

Following his recent win over Tim Henman, Andrew completed the double over his British compatriots with a victory against Greg Rusedski in the Aberdeen Cup.

Joined by brother Jamie, he led the Scots to success over England in the inaugural event.

And to cap a stunning 2005 he won the Glenfiddich Spirit of Scotland Award for sport last week, joining previous winners Colin Montgomerie, David Coulthard and Alex Ferguson.

Andrew was unable to be present for the awards ceremony but his mother Judy collected the award on his behalf.

She accepted the award from Menstrie's double Olympic gold winner Shirley Robertson, saying: "Any time he has to wear a shirt and tie for something, he always seems to get out of it."

2 Select six headings from the list below to use as section headings for your essay plan.

> Childhood   Hobbies and interests
> Sporting achievements   Diet
> How Andy became interested in tennis   Lifestyle
> Success in 2005   Injuries
>   Family

3 Write two or three bullet points summarising what you will include under each heading.

4 Which paragraph would you use at the beginning of your essay, following your introduction? Why?

5 Which three of the sections above did you **not** include in your plan? Why?

Activity 2

The text below is the introduction to a magazine article by another student. Check for any errors in sentence structure, punctuation and spelling. The first line is chatty and informal, to appeal to young people. Can you improve the tone of the rest of the piece to appeal to a teenage reader? Copy out the text, then annotate it to mark up any errors and changes you would want to make.

So how many of you dream of being a sporting hero? Andrew Murray is the highest ranked tennis player every produced by scotland and in addition is currently the highest ranked British player While still a teenager he achieved some remarkable victories over other leading tennis players, including notably, argubly the world's best tennis player Roager Federer.

Activity 3

A topic sentence in a non-fiction text expresses the main idea of each paragraph. It is usually the first sentence of the paragraph and explains what the paragraph is about.

Below is a plan for an essay on Andy Murray's life. Write a topic sentence to begin each paragraph, based on your reading. The first one has been done for you.

How he began playing tennis

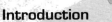

Murray's childhood and family

Introduction
Andy Murray is the highest ranked tennis player Scotland has ever produced. Currently, he is also Britain's best tennis player.

Other sports he enjoys

Tennis achievements

His training and diet

Knowledge about language: Formal and informal language – contractions

- Contractions are when two words such as 'he is' or 'do not' are shortened into one with apostrophes to indicate where letters have been missed out ('he's', 'don't').
- They are used in speech and when a writer wants to create an informal, chatty effect.
- They would not normally be used in formal writing.

Look again at the texts in Activities 1 and 2 (pages 18–20). Which texts use contractions and which do not?

List all the contractions you find and, next to them, write down the two words each contraction comes from, e.g. *don't = do not*.

Reading Activity
Reading for information

Steve Irwin, Crocodile Hunter

Steve Irwin is well known for his work with crocodiles and other animals. In 2006, he was stung by a bull ray fish and died.

You have been asked to do some research on Steve Irwin for a book about people who are well known for their work with animals. You have been given various texts about Irwin, which you can use for your research.

Your task

Look at texts A–E on pages 23–29, then do the activities below.

1 Skim through the texts. Briefly explain what kind each one is and how you can tell.

2 Scan Text C. Find and write down:
   a two facts about Steve Irwin
   b two opinions about Steve Irwin.

3 **a** Say which text you think is going to be **most** helpful to you and explain why.
   b Say which text is going to be **least** helpful to you and explain why.

4 Choose one text that you think presents Steve Irwin in a **positive** way and explain how the text does this. In your answer, comment on:
   ● the choice of information included about Irwin
   ● the choice of language used to describe him and what he did
   ● other techniques used to convey a particular view of him.

5 Choose one text that you think presents Steve Irwin in a **negative** way and explain how the text does this. In your answer comment on:
   ● the choice of information included about Irwin
   ● the choice of language used to describe him and what he did
   ● other techniques used to convey a particular view of him.

6 What impressions do you get of Steve Irwin as a person from the texts? Support your answer with quotations from at least two of them.

7 Make notes of the main points you want to include in your biography of Steve Irwin, and organise them into paragraphs. You can decide whether you want to present him in a positive or a negative way – or present a balanced point of view about him. You can decide how you want to organise your notes.

CAIRNS, Australia – Wildlife warrior Steve Irwin was a daredevil who loved flirting with danger around deadly animals.

But after years of close shaves it was a normally harmless stingray which finally claimed his life on Monday, plunging a barb into the Crocodile Hunter's chest as he snorkelled in shallow water on the Great Barrier Reef.

The 44-year-old TV personality may have died instantly when struck by the stingray while filming a sequence for his eight-year-old daughter Bindi's new TV series, *Friends Believe*.

'You think about all the documentaries we've made and all the dangerous situations that we have been in, you always think "is this it, is this a day that may be his demise?",' said his friend

> **"He didn't have a fear of death at all."**

and manager John Stainton. '[But] nothing would ever scare Steve or would worry him. He didn't have a fear of death at all.'

Mr Irwin made his international reputation wrestling crocodiles and snakes. But the flamboyant naturalist's final confrontation with a wild animal occurred at Batt Reef off Port Douglas on Monday morning, where he had been filming a new documentary, *Ocean's Deadliest*.

Taking time off from the main project, Mr Irwin was swimming in shallow water, snorkelling as his cameraman filmed large bull rays.

'He came over the top of a stingray and the stingray's barb went up and went into his chest and put a hole into his heart,' said Mr Irwin's friend and manager John Stainton.

'It's likely that he possibly died instantly when the barb hit him, and I don't think that he ... felt any pain.'

Wildlife experts said the normally passive creatures only sting in defence, striking with a bayonet-like barb when they feel threatened.

Unconscious, Mr Irwin was pulled aboard his research vessel, *Croc One*, for a 30-minute dash to Low Isle, where an emergency helicopter had been summoned at about 11 a.m., his Australia Zoo said in a statement.

The crew of the *Croc One* performed constant CPR during the voyage to Low Isle, but medical staff pronounced Mr Irwin dead about noon.

His wife Terri was told of her husband's death while on a walking tour in Tasmania, and returned to the Sunshine Coast with her two children, Bindi and three-year-old son Bob.

The death of the larger than life Mr Irwin, best known for his catchcry 'Crikey!', caused shockwaves around the world, leading TV bulletins in the United States and Britain.

Mr Irwin was also a global phenomenon, making almost 50 documentaries which appeared on the cable TV channel Animal Planet, and which generated books, interactive games and even toy action figures.

Prime Minister John Howard said: 'I am quite shocked and distressed at Steve Irwin's sudden, untimely and freakish death. It's a huge loss to Australia.

'He was a wonderful character. He was a passionate environmentalist. He brought joy and entertainment and excitement to millions of people.'

"He was a passionate environmentalist. He brought joy and entertainment to millions of people."

The Melbourne-born father of two's *Crocodile Hunter* programme was first broadcast in 1992 and has been shown around the world on cable network Discovery.

He also starred in movies and helped develop the Australia Zoo wildlife park, north of Brisbane, which was started by his parents Bob and Lyn Irwin.

He grew up near crocodiles, trapping and removing them from populated areas and releasing them in his parents' park, which he took over in 1991.

Bob was involved in a controversial incident in January 2004, when his father held his infant son in one arm as he fed a dead chicken to a crocodile at Australia Zoo.

Child-welfare and animal-rights groups criticised his actions as irresponsible and tantamount to child abuse.

Mr Irwin said any danger to his son was only a perceived danger and that he was in complete control of the situation.

In June 2004, Mr Irwin came under fire again when it was alleged he came too close to and disturbed some whales, seals and penguins while filming a documentary in Antarctica.

Mr Irwin was also a tourism ambassador and was heavily involved in last year's 'G'Day LA' tourism campaign.

Queensland Premier Peter Beattie said Mr Irwin was an 'extraordinary man'.

'He has made an enormous difference to his state and his country,' he said.

From the *Sydney Morning Herald* 4 September 2006

STEVE WASN'T GOING TO DIE IN BED

BY VIRGINIA WHEELER
5 SEPTEMBER 2006

Irwin, wife Terri and a croc

WILDLIFE expert David Bellamy last night told of his grief at the loss of Crocodile Hunter Steve Irwin – but said: 'He was never going to die quietly in his bed.'

The British botanist called Aussie icon Irwin – killed by a stingray while snorkelling yesterday – a 'fantastic all-action character'.

He said: 'I had a good cry when I heard the terrible news. Why did it happen to such an important and talented guy? It is the world's loss and has sadly come years too early.'

Outrageous Irwin, 44, won global TV fame by leaping on the backs of giant crocodiles and grabbing deadly snakes while crowing in a broad Aussie accent: 'Crikey! Look at this little bewdy.'

Though one of the world's top naturalists, many of his millions of fans feared he would eventually be killed taking one chance too many with a croc.

But he died while filming a bull ray in shallow water at Batt Reef, a remote part of the Great Barrier Reef in northern Queensland.

The 5ft-wide ray, normally a placid creature, suddenly turned on him and speared him through the heart with a lash from the toxic barb on its tail.

A plume of blood filled the crystal-clear reef water. And dad-of-two Irwin – universally loved for his childlike enthusiasm, khaki shorts and huge boots – died almost instantly.

Last night it was unclear if he was killed by the wound, a heart attack, poison from the blade-like barb or a combination of all three.

Paramedics tried in vain to revive him and he was pronounced dead on his boat, *Croc One.*

His death was caught on film by a cameraman from his production company, who was swimming in front of him.

The footage was being studied by police last night. Irwin always told film crews to keep shooting even if it looked like he was going to come off worst in a croc or shark attack.

His best friend and manager John Stainton, who witnessed the tragedy, wept as he said: 'Steve would have been sad if he died and it wasn't captured on camera.

'He died doing what he loved best and left this world in a happy and peaceful state of mind. I hope he never felt any pain. The world has lost a great wildlife icon, a passionate conservationist and one of the proudest dads on the planet.

'His last words would have been, "Crocs rule!"'

Irwin's American wife Terri, daughter Bindi, eight, and son Bob, three, were on holiday in Tasmania when they learned of his death.

They flew to Queensland last night and headed for the family home at Minyama on the state's Sunshine Coast.

Text D

In late October 2000, writer Sarah Simpson from magazine *Scientific American* finds herself seated at a table in Steve Irwin's childhood home. The Crocodile Hunter himself sits across from her, explaining how his father built this house in 1970. Now it has become one of the administrative buildings for Australia Zoo, which Irwin's parents established and which he now directs together with his wife, Terri.

SCIENTIFIC AMERICAN: Why do you think you're so popular?

STEVE: Nothing to do with my looks, that's for sure! [laughing] Yeah, I normally get a big croc out in the foreground of any filming.

You know what I reckon it is? My belief is that what comes across on the television is a capture of my enthusiasm and my passion for wildlife. Since I was a boy, from this house, I was out rescuing crocodiles and snakes. My mum and dad were very passionate about that and I was lucky enough to go along. The first crocodile I ever caught was at nine years of age, and it was a rescue. So now what happens is the cameras follow me around and capture exactly what I've been doing since I was a boy. Only now we have a team of, you know, like 73 of us, and it's gone beyond that.

As the audience, I want you to come with me, right? So we get cameras, every one of us, if we've got a four- or five-man film crew, including myself and Terri. Every one of us can use a camera. I have one in my green backpack that I pull out for the hard-core shots where you've gotta get right in there, so the camera's always right there, in there, while I'm doing my thing. So when I'm talking to the camera, I'm talking to *you*, in your living room.

We've evolved from sitting back on our tripods and shooting wildlife films like they have been shot historically, which doesn't work for us. So, now it's not just, 'Oh look, there's a cheetah making a kill.' I want to take you to the cheetah. I want to get in there as close as I can to that cheetah. You'll see me in Namibia getting attacked by a female cheetah, because I didn't know she had cubs, but the cameras are right there in a four-wheel-drive, filming me. She's 'grrraagh!' putting mock-charges on, and you get that overwhelming sensation that you're there, that you're with me.

SA: And what do you think your zany attitude does for the viewers?

STEVE: It excites them, which helps me to educate. I believe that education is all about being excited about something. Seeing passion and enthusiasm helps to push an educational message. That's the main aim in our entire lives – to promote education about wildlife and wilderness areas, save habitats, save endangered species, etc. So, if we can get people excited about animals, then by crikey, it makes it a heck of a lot easier to save them.

My field is with apex predators, hence your crocodiles, your snakes, your spiders. And then of course you've got lions, tigers, bears. Great big apex predators – they're the species that I enjoy the most. That's where my passion lies. Historically, people have seen them as evil, ugly monsters that kill people. Take the crocodile, for example, my favourite animal. There are 23 species. Seventeen of those species are rare or endangered. They're on the way out, no matter what anyone does or says, you know.

So, my tactic with conservation of apex predators is to get people excited and take them to where they live.

Text E

The real crocodile hunter

By Germaine Greer
5 September 2006

The world mourns. World-famous wildlife warrior Steve Irwin has died a hero, doing the thing he loved, filming a sequence for a new TV series. He was supposed to have been making a new documentary to have been called *Ocean's Deadliest*. But, when filming was held up by bad weather, he decided to 'go off and shoot a few segments' for his 8 year-old daughter's upcoming TV series. His manager John Stainton just said 'Fine, anything that would keep him moving and keep his adrenaline going.' Evidently it's Stainton's job to keep Irwin pumped larger than life, shouting 'Crikey!' and punching the air.

Irwin was the real Crocodile Dundee, a great Australian, an ambassador for wildlife, a global **phenomenon**. The only creatures he couldn't dominate were parrots. A parrot once did its best to rip his nose off his face.

What seems to have happened is that Irwin and a cameraman went off in a little dinghy to see what they

Irwin tosses chicken to a crocodile while holding his baby son

could find. What they found were stingrays. You can just imagine Irwin yelling: 'Just look at these beauties! Crikey! With those barbs a stingray can kill a horse!' All Australian children know that stingrays bury themselves in the sand or mud with only their eyes sticking out. What you don't do with a stingray is stand on it. The lashing response of the tail is automatic; the barb is coated with a deadly slime.

As a Melbourne boy, Irwin should have had a healthy respect for stingrays. The film-makers maintain that the ray that took Irwin out was a 'bull ray', but this is not usually found as far north as Port Douglas. **Marine biologist** Dr Meredith Peach has been quoted as saying, 'It's really quite unusual for divers to be stung unless they are grappling with the animal and, knowing Steve Irwin, perhaps that may have been the case.'

The only time Irwin ever seemed less than entirely lovable to his fans (as distinct from **zoologists**) was when he went into the Australia Zoo crocodile enclosure with his month-old baby son in one hand and a dead chicken in the other. For a second you didn't know which one he meant to feed to the crocodile. If the crocodile had been less depressed it might have made the decision for him. As the dozy beast obediently downed its tiny snack, Irwin walked his baby on the grass, not something that **paediatricians** recommend for rubbery baby legs even when there isn't a stir-crazy carnivore a few feet away. The adoring world was momentarily appalled. They called it child abuse. The whole spectacle was revolting.

Irwin's response to the sudden outburst of criticism was bizarre. He believed that he had the crocodile under control. But he could have fallen over, suggested an interviewer. He admitted that was possible, but only if a meteor had hit the earth and caused an earthquake of 6.6 on the **Richter scale**.

What Irwin never seemed to understand was that animals need space. The one lesson any conservationist must try to drive home is that habitat loss is the principal cause of species loss. There was no habitat, no matter how fragile or finely balanced, that Irwin hesitated to barge into. There was not an animal he was not prepared to manhandle. Every creature he brandished at the camera was in distress. Every snake badgered by Irwin was at a huge disadvantage, with only a single possible reaction to its terrifying situation, which was to strike. But Irwin was an entertainer, a 21st-century version of a lion-tamer, with crocodiles instead of lions.

Explanations

phenomenon **remarkable person**
marine biologist **scientist who studies the sea**
zoologists **scientists who study animals**
paediatricians **doctors of children's diseases**
Richter scale **measurement scale for earthquakes named after its creator Dr Charles Francis Richter.**

Writing Activity
functional writing

Steve Irwin, Crocodile Hunter

Your task

You have been asked to write a biography of Steve Irwin. You have read and studied texts about him and made some notes. If you like, you can include some information and opinions from other material you find yourself. You can choose whether you present him in a positive way or a negative way – or present a balanced point of view about him.

You should:

- organise your points logically into paragraphs or sections with subheadings and provide an effective beginning and ending

- use a variety of sentence structures and remember to link your ideas using a range of connectives.

- use capital letters, full stops and commas accurately to make your writing clear for the reader.

2 News

Experiences and outcomes

In this unit you will:

Reading
- infer and deduce meaning using evidence from the text
- identify how a media text suits its audience
- scan for facts and recognise opinion
- recognise how print and images combine to create meaning.

Writing
- evaluate an event and present findings from a personal point of view
- recognise and use four different kinds of sentence

Talking and Listening
- present a news story so that listeners can follow it
- give clearly linked answers, instructions and explanations
- put across a point of view with supporting evidence.

Punctuation and spelling
- use exclamation marks to reinforce meaning
- use apostrophes of possession.

By the end of this unit you will:
- present a news story
  (Talking and Listening Activity: Group discussion)
- read and answer questions on a news article
  (Reading Activity: Close reading).

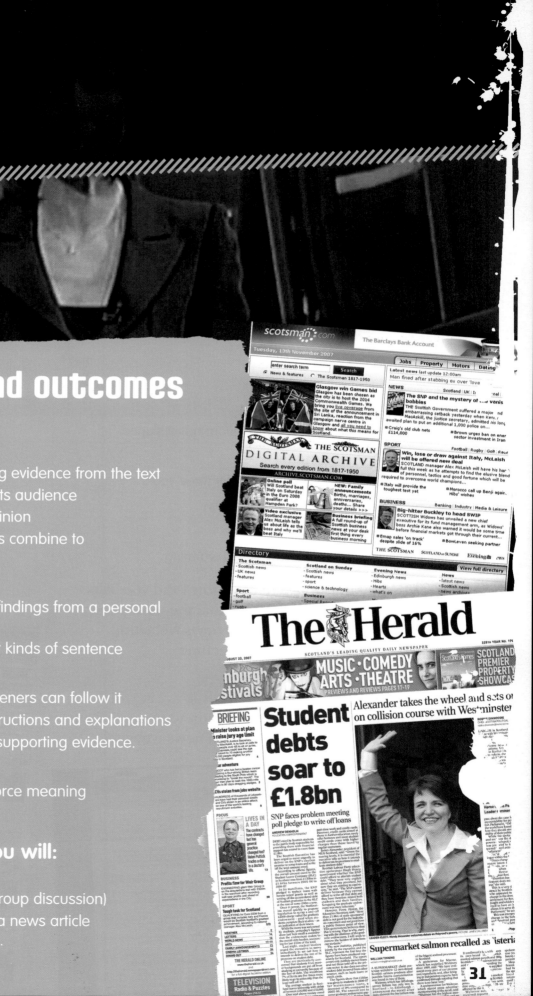

1 Presenting the news

You are learning:
- what makes the news, the different forms it takes, and how we choose to get it.

The news is all around us. Events and incidents are always happening and the news is being updated constantly. A hundred years ago the only way to get the news was by reading a newspaper; today, people can access the news when and how they want it.

Activity 1

1. Which of the stories in the table below would you put in a UK national newspaper, television news report or news website, and which would you not use at all?

	National newspaper	TV news	News website	I would not use it
The Prime Minister of the United Kingdom has resigned				
Scotland win 6–0				
Film star reveals she has been single for three years				
Open-air swimming pool may close down				
Woman, aged 56, gives birth to triplets				
Scientists warn: act now to slow global warming				

2. **a** Which of the stories in question 1 did you select for inclusion in all three media: the newspaper, the television news and the news website?

   b Which stories did you not include in all three? Why not?

3. Write a sentence beginning 'News is …', in which you explain the kind of information we can get from newspapers, television news and news websites.

Activity 2

1 Different media present the news in different ways for different people. What are the advantages and disadvantages of newspapers, television news and news websites? Think about:
- how and when people can access them
- how much news they provide
- how much the reader or viewer can choose which stories to find out about.

2 Which media – television news, newspaper or news website – would you recommend for the people below?

I want to know everything that's going on. I can spend hours finding out all about the latest stories and events in the world.

Craig

We want a quick summary of all the news after the kids are in bed but we're usually too tired to read by then.

Donald and Emily

I'm very busy. The only time I can catch up on the news is in taxis or on trains. I'm mainly interested in financial and political news.

Marie

3 Look carefully at the images on page 32. They are from Sky News, *The Herald* newspaper and *The Scotsman* website.

How would you describe the newsreader and the newsroom, the newspaper front page and the news website? Why have they been presented in this way?

2 Features of a newspaper front page

You are learning:
- to explore the layout of a newspaper front page and how to write an effective headline.

The front page of a newspaper needs to be bold and eyecatching. It uses distinct features to achieve this.

Activity 1

Masthead
The name and logo of the newspaper

Puff
An eye-catching graphic to advertise what else can be found inside the newspaper

Headline
Sums up the main newspaper story to attract and intrigue the reader

Image
A picture to illustrate the article

Byline
Tells the reader who wrote the article

Text
The main body of the article, telling the story in detail

Strapline
Adds a little more detail to the headline

1 Which of the layout features identified above does the following?
   a Clearly and boldly shows the name of the newspaper.
   b Tempts the reader to buy the newspaper with things on offer inside.
   c Encourages the reader to read the story on the front page by summing it up in as few words as possible.
   d Gives more information about the headline.
   e Says who the journalist is.
   f Givest more detailed information, including facts and quotes.
   g Makes the front page more visually appealing.

Activity 2

An effective headline should sum up the news story and attract attention, making the reader want to find out more.

1   Look at the headline for the news story on page 34. Write down two or more reasons to explain why you think the headline writer chose it.

2   Here are some rules for effective headline writing. A good headline:
- summarises the story in as few words as possible
- leaves out unnecessary words like 'the' or 'a'
- is often written in the present tense
- often uses dramatic or **emotive** language
- sometimes uses a play on words or **pun**
- sometimes uses **alliteration**: two or more words beginning with the same sound or letter.

Which rules do these headlines follow?

A *Daily Record*, **Tuesday 21 August 2007, p17**

YOU NEARLY COPT IT THERE

This woman's relief was short lived after she was rescued from floods in Oklahoma.

A news crew filmed the woman being plucked to safety from a rooftop by a highway patrol helicopter – then dropped back into the floodwater.

B *The Herald*, **Tuesday 21 August 2007, p5**

BLAZE HOTEL BOSS TELLS OF 'PANIC'

The manager of a seaside hotel destroyed by fire said last night he was totally distraught after the fatal blaze.

Andy Woollam was called to the Penhallow Hotel in Newquay, Cornwall, as soon as the fire started just after midnight on Saturday.

Two people are still unaccounted for and four are in hospital following the fire that killed one man.

C *Daily Record*, **Wednesday 22 August 2007, p2**

TOP COP JOB RACE

Intelligence expert and a top English policeman are the frontrunners to replace the out-going chief of 'Scotland's FBI'

Graeme Pearson, director general of the Scottish Crime and Drug Enforcement Agency, will retire from his £100,000-a-year post in November.

D *Daily Record*, **Tuesday 21 August 2007, p2**

Brown on the ball

Gordon Brown and German Chancellor Angela Merkel will watch England play Germany at Wembley tomorrow.

Activity 3

1   Use the table below to help you select the best words to create the most effective headline for this story.

A school is so infested with rats, they are invading classrooms during lessons and frightening students.

rat	infested	school	frightens	students
rodent	filled	lessons	terrifies	pupils
animal	riddled	classroom	scares	children

2   Which of the headline rules have you used? Write two or three sentences explaining how you have made your headline effective.

Self-evaluation

1   Design a newspaper front page for the headline you wrote in Activity 3. Remember to include all the features you explored in Activity 1.

2   Write a list of all the features you have included in your front page.

3   Write a sentence or two for each feature, explaining the effect you were trying to create.

3 Structure of a newspaper article

You are learning:

- how the information in a newspaper article is organised by exploring the structure of an article and planning your own.

A newspaper article isn't just a story, it's a carefully crafted information text, with its own style and way of using language.

Activity 1

1 Read this newspaper story, then complete tasks **a–e** below to help you understand how the information in the article has been organised.

15 August 2007

Rover's Return after six years

By Stuart MacDonald

A family are celebrating the return of their runaway dog – more than SIX YEARS after he went missing.

Collie cross Quincy did a bunk from his family's front garden in April 2001.

Owners Colin and Audrey Smith never stopped missing him and their autistic son Lewis kept asking where he had gone.

And they were amazed when staff at an animal shelter turned up to tell them Quincy had been found.

Quincy was discovered in the street in the centre of Glasgow last week. He was cold and starving.

He was taken to a shelter where staff found details of his owners after scanning a microchip implanted under his skin.

Audrey, 41, said, 'When the staff from the shelter turned up with a photo of him, Lewis started shouting, "That's Quincy! That's Quincy!"

'He was ecstatic; because of his autism, he had grown very attached to Quincy and was very upset when he went missing.'

Colin, 43, said, 'It's remarkable that Quincy has finally come home.'

a Write down:

- **who** was involved
- **when** it happened
- **why** it happened.
- **what** happened
- **where** it happened

b Which paragraphs give you all this information?

c What information do the other paragraphs give?

d Why has the writer included quotations from the family?

e How many sentences are there in each paragraph? Why do you think the writer has done this?

2 Write a set of instructions on structuring a newspaper article. Use these sentence starters to help you.

- The first one or two paragraphs of a newspaper article should tell the reader ...
- The middle paragraphs of a newspaper article should ...
- The writer often includes quotations to ...
- The final paragraph of a newspaper article usually ...
- The number of sentences in each paragraph can vary but often ...

Activity 2

You are a newspaper reporter. You have been given the information opposite and told to write an article for tomorrow's front page.

Follow steps 1–4 below to prepare a role-play in which you will interview the key characters to find out the facts of the case.

International pop star Buster Bling has been arrested. The police say he is accused of stealing his girlfriend's pet budgie. His girlfriend is called Donna Bellissimo. The budgie's name is Derek.

17366

1   Decide which characters you will interview. You should talk to Buster Bling, Donna Bellissimo and the police. You could also interview Buster's solicitor or even get a budgie expert's comments.

2   Before you begin your interviews, you need to plan what each character is like, what they know and what they think. Use the points below to help you.

   a   Write down two or three words to describe the personality and attitudes of each character in the story.

   b   Write a short biography – two or three sentences – for each character.

   c   What do they think of the other people involved?

   d   What were they doing at the time the budgie went missing?

   e   Why do they think this might have happened?

3   Plan the questions you will ask your interviewees, then plan their answers.

4   Rehearse and perform your role-play.

> Remember: the most important thing in a role-play is to sustain, or keep up, your role. Don't laugh or stop being the character you are playing. What would you think if a film actor did that in the middle of a movie?

Activity 3

The editor of your newspaper wants the Buster Bling story on the front page with a large headline and a big picture of Buster. You have only six paragraphs to write your Buster Bling story. What will you put in each paragraph? Use the instructions you wrote in Activity 1 to help you plan the structure of your article.

4 Aiming at a target audience

You are learning:
- how newspaper stories are chosen to suit their readers and how different newspapers tell the same stories in different ways.

Local newspapers don't usually include the national news – politics, international affairs, major sporting events – unless it has something to do with the area in which the local newspaper is sold. Local newspapers are full of local news, aimed at local readers.

Activity 1

1 Which do you think these headlines might have been taken from – local or national newspapers?

(A) **Ice rink to re-open before Christmas**

(E) **Ten new jobs at biscuit factory**

(B) **Rugovian president to meet Brown at No.10**

(F) **More Britons buying holiday homes abroad than ever before**

(C) ***Thousands of bank notes could be forgeries**

(G) **New toys for toddler playgroup**

(D) **Aberdeen win again – and again**

(H) **Community police officer retires after 30 years' service**

2 Choose four of these headlines – two from a local newspaper and two from a national newspaper. Write an explanation of how you decided which kind of newspaper they were from.

Activity 2

Here are the headlines and opening paragraphs of two articles from two Scottish national newspapers. They tell the same story but are written in very different ways. Answer questions 1–6 to explore the differences and how the newspapers aim for different audiences.

Daily Record, Friday, 7 September 2007

Salt risk for kids

Kids with a high salt diet are risking heart disease in adulthood, doctors fear.

The worry is prompted by a study's findings that kids who eat a lot of salt have higher blood pressure.

One expert said it was particularly disturbing as the vast majority of British kids eat far too much salt.

Research published in *The Journal of Human Hypertension* found that just an extra gram of salt a day leads to significant rises in blood pressure.

Preventative medicine expert Professor Malcolm Law said: 'Higher blood pressure is a marker of vascular damage and this shows it's starting too early.

'The products targeted by the food industry at children, including baby food, have too much salt.'

CHILDREN'S SALT LEVEL LINKED WITH HIGH BLOOD PRESSURE

Health campaigners today urged parents to check food for salt content after research revealed children with higher salt diets have higher blood pressure.

Analysis of the diets of more than 1600 youngsters found a strong link between salt intake and systolic blood pressure after factors such as age, sex and body mass index were taken into account.

The research, based on data collected in the National Diet and Nutrition Survey (NDNS) for young people in Great Britain, and published in the *Journal of Hypertension*, backs the findings of earlier salt reduction trials in children and young people.

A total of 2127 children aged between four and 18 were involved in the NDNS carried out in 1997.

The Herald
Friday, 7 September 2007

1 Write a summary of this story in one sentence.

2 When do the two articles tell the reader the main point of the story?

3 Compare the two articles' headlines. Would you describe their language as formal or informal? Which uses more emotive or dramatic language?

4 Compare the language in both articles. Which one uses more formal language? Give some examples.

5 Write two or three sentences summing up the differences between these two articles.

6 What kinds of readers do you think these two newspapers are trying to appeal to?

Knowledge about language: Sentence types

There are four different sentence types.

Statement: a sentence that states a fact or an opinion and is either true or false. It ends with a full stop, for example, 'I like cheese.' or 'Three plus four makes seven.'
Question: a sentence that asks for a response. It ends with a question mark, e.g.: 'Are you ready yet?'
Command: a sentence that gives an instruction or makes a request. It can end with a full stop or an exclamation mark, for example: 'Boil for ten minutes.' or 'Sit down!'
Exclamation: a sentence used to express a strong feeling. It always ends with an exclamation mark, for example, 'Oh my goodness!' or 'Ouch!'

What kinds of sentences are these?

1 You should only cross the road at a zebra crossing.
2 Can you be sure that a driver has seen you?
3 Drivers never pay enough attention to pedestrians.
4 Do you always do that?
5 Be safe!
6 Idiots!

5 Close reading

You are learning:

● how journalists give us more than just the facts. You will learn to scan for facts, identify opinions and read between the lines.

You are often asked to read a text and answer questions about it. An effective way of retrieving this information is to identify a key word in the question – a word that is important – and scan the text for it. This means you do not have to re-read the whole text – you can just look for the word you need to help you answer the question.

Activity 1

In question 1 below the key words are *crash diet*. Scan the article to find them. This will lead you to the answer.

The Labradors too fat to go for a walk

Flabradors Tasha and Heidi are being forced to go on a crash diet to save their lives – after ballooning to a whopping SEVEN stone each.

The plump pooches piled on the pounds by wolfing down 1000 grams of dog food a day – twice the recommended amount – on top of fatty snacks.

To make matters worse, the 10 year-old sisters were hardly ever walked by their last owner, who has recently signed them over to the RSPCA.

They are left panting and out of breath after just a few minutes on their paws and when they attempt to run or jump their coats ripple with fat.

Officers are so worried their hind legs will buckle under the huge bulk that they have put them on a strict weight-loss plan to get them down to the normal three-and-a-half stone.

Most Labradors live to the age of 14, but Tasha and Heidi may not reach that age because they are in such a poor state of health.

RSPCA Centre manager Nikki Smith said: 'We are saddened by the state of these dogs as it clearly shows they have not had the exercise they need for many months.

'With guidance from our vet they are given short spells of exercise in the centre dog run where they can be carefully monitored.

'But sadly unless they can shed a few pounds, they may not reach their full life span of 14 years because their weight does put extra strain on their hearts.

'We just want to remind dog owners that it's vital to keep an eye on their pets' health – and not kill them with kindness.'

1 Why have the dogs been put on a crash diet?

2 How much dog food were the dogs used to eating?

3 How often were the dogs walked by their last owner?

4 What is the normal weight for a Labrador?

5 What is the full life span for a Labrador?

Activity 2

A fact is something that can be proved to be true. An opinion is what someone thinks or believes – other people may disagree.

You shouldn't believe every word you read. You need to be able to tell the difference between what is true and what is just the writer's opinion.

1 Which of these statements taken from the article are facts and which are opinions?
   a The dogs weigh seven stone.
   b The dogs are ten years old.
   c The dogs will not live as long as they should.
   d The dogs are huge.

2 Write down three facts and three opinions about your school.

Activity 3

Sometimes the writer's opinion is not clearly stated. It is suggested or implied by the words the writer uses. You need to read between the lines to work out the writer's opinion. Read this sentence from the article again:

> The plump pooches piled on the pounds by wolfing down 1000 grams of dog food a day – twice the recommended amount – on top of fatty snacks.

1 There are some facts in this sentence. What are they?

2 The writer adds his opinion to the facts through his choice of language. What do these words suggest or imply about the writer's opinion: *plump, piled on, wolfing, fatty*?

3 a Write down three other words from the article the writer has used to suggest this opinion.
   b Are these words formal or informal?

4 What do these words suggest about the writer's attitude to this story? Does the writer think it is funny or worrying that the dogs are so overweight?

Self-evaluation

How confident are you about the skills you have practised in these activities? Assess yourself using the grid below.

	I can't do this ✓	I think I can do this ✓	I can definitely do this ✓
I can scan a text for key words and retrieve information.			
I can identify the writer's opinion implied by the words the writer chooses.			
I can imply an opinion in my own writing through the words I choose.			

6 Recounting events

You are learning:
● to explore a television news report and practise your recount skills.

Television news gives information in different ways from a newspaper. They use different techniques to be effective, which also means the same story may end up creating very different feelings and reactions from the two audiences.

Activity 1

Read the transcript below of a television news report and then answer the questions to help you explore television news.

Whale remains stuck in Fraserburgh harbour

News reporter:

Well, the latest is it's moved from the mouth of the harbour to this area around here behind me which has made it easier to see, so the public's been down here, causing – it's become something of an attraction. They're not the only ones whale watching today though: scientists have been keeping a close eye on it since it arrived yesterday afternoon after apparently following a fishing boat into the harbour. Now they reckon it's about 5m long. Minke whales reach about 10m, so they think it might just be a little baby around 4 or 5 months old. They're worried that all this commotion might be causing it some anxiety. However, there doesn't appear to be any sign of stress at the moment.

Interviewee 1:

At the moment, yeah, she doesn't seem to be showing any signs of distress. Generally the ones that end somewhat sadly are ones that beach themselves. She hasn't actually beached herself – she's just got herself stuck where she can't get out. So she's still in, you know, she's still swimming in the water so she's happy.

1 What are the main differences in the presentation and delivery of news in a newspaper article and a television news item?

2 Is the language used in this news report formal or informal? Write down three examples to support your answer.

3 What does this language suggest about the newsreader's opinion? Does the newsreader think it is funny or worrying that the whale is stranded?

4 How do the newsreader's voice and facial expressions help to express this opinion?

5 Try reading the transcript as if you were a newsreader, but using a different tone of voice and facial expressions to give a different opinion. What is the effect?

Activity 2

1 Re-read the news transcript. What are the key points of this story? Try to sum up the story in five short sentences, keeping all the important information. Remember: the key points of a news story are often *who*, *what*, *when*, *why* and *where*.

2 Add one more key information point, making a total of six short sentences. Write a short explanation of why you chose that point.

3 Without looking, recount this story to a partner. Ask your partner to check you have included all the key information. Then swap roles.

Activity 3

The aim of this activity is to work in a group, helping each other to complete the task.

1 Choose a news headline from the suggestions here. Working in your group, make up the details of the story and prepare a brief account of it for broadcast on television news. Remember: your viewers will want to know at least the five key points of the story: *who*, *what*, *when*, *why* and *where*.

2 Write a short evaluation of your group work. Try to comment on:
- how well you worked as a team
- how you could help a group to work together more effectively next time.

Genius six-year-old beats world champion

Socks fetch record price on Internet auction

Teenage lottery winner buys school

Parrot foils burglars

School-trip teacher stranded on desert island for three years

Talking and Listening Activity
Group discussion

The hamster story

You are a news team working for a local television company. You are given news stories and have to develop an item for the daily local television news, which goes out at 6 pm. You are given the news story below.

Lonely hamster does a runner

Hammy, a 9-month-old hamster, escaped from his cage in Class 4 at Braeview Primary School during the October holiday. Janitor Jim Smith discovered the school pet was missing on Thursday and had to break the news to tearful youngsters who returned to school on Monday. 'First I knew was when I spotted the cage door was ajar,' said Mr Smith, 55, who has been janitor at the school for 15 years.

Patsy Jones, teacher in charge of Primary 4, claimed the cage had been securely shut when she left school the previous Friday. Hammy was supposed to be spending the holiday with one of the children but in the rush to get away, Hammy was forgotten and so had to spend a lonely week on his own.

Local vet Alex McKay said: 'Hamsters are nervous creatures and you can't blame him for taking the opportunity to escape while he could.' This incident has raised the question of whether schools should be allowed to keep animals. Chris Jenkins of the local animal rights group SAVE said: 'This is exactly why people – and schools are included in this – should *not* be allowed to have pets. We are campaigning for keeping pets to be made illegal.'

However, child psychologist Sam Pepper told our reporter that looking after animals was one of the best ways of teaching children about responsibility. The debate goes on. Meanwhile, if you come across a hamster on the run, who can't find his way home, please phone our news desk on 01487 923710.

In your group you need:

A newsreader

A reporter at the scene of the escape

An interviewer

You can include some of the following:

- Jim Smith, the janitor
- Patsy Jones, Primary 4 teacher
- Chris Jenkins from SAVE
- Sam Pepper, the child psychologist
- Alex Mckay, the local vet.

Your task

Create a news item for television based on this news story. You can decide the final format of your news story, but you should include as many of the following as possible:

- reporting the facts
- outside reporting from the scene of the escape
- interviews with people involved
- discussion with 'experts'
- comments from people in the street.

If you are reading the news, interviewing or chairing a discussion, you can have some written questions to work from. Otherwise, you have to think beforehand what your character would think and feel and say. Try to:

- make each character distinctly different
- explore some of the issues raised by this story
- create an entertaining news item for the audience.

You will be assessed on:

- how well you work in a group, building on the ideas of other people to get the task done
- how well you listen to other people and show this in what you say
- how well you sustain your role in the news story.

7 Point of view

You are learning:
- how writers express a point of view, developing your understanding of how language can imply an opinion.

In the same way that writers try to influence an audience by choosing which facts and opinions to give you, the careful use of words can subtly imply the opinion of the writer to try to influence you further.

Activity 1

1   Read the news story below.

Classroom thugs told: Disrupt school and win an iPod!

School tearaways in England are to be offered mountain bikes and iPods in return for good behaviour.

In a Westminster government campaign against soaring indiscipline, teachers are being told to reward disruptive pupils with prizes and privileges.

Badly behaved youngsters must be praised five times as often as they are punished or criticised, under guidelines unveiled by Education Secretary Alan Johnson.

They can be offered prizes and privileges ranging from non-uniform days and extended breaktimes to CDs, cinema tickets, personal music players and state-of-the-art bicycles.

The scheme has been branded 'absurd'.

Ministers were accused of 'going soft' on discipline, and critics said the guidance would encourage pupils to expect prizes for good behaviour that should be considered the norm.

Chris Woodhead, the former chief inspector of schools, said: 'As a taxpayer, I would like to know how much this absurd guidance cost – it is a complete irrelevance to the real world.'

Tory education spokesman David Willetts said: 'Children have a very strong sense of fairness. It will be resented if it looks as if bad behaviour brings rewards.'

The new government advice states that pupils should be given five rewards for every criticism or punishment.

Minister's latest bright idea for curbing school thugs is to reward them

'It has long been established that rewards are more effective than punishment in motivating pupils,' the guidelines say.

'By praising and rewarding positive behaviour, others will be encouraged to act similarly.'

Teachers are warned not to impose whole-class detentions or other sanctions that punish the innocent as well as the guilty.

And they are told: 'Staff should also consider when it might be more appropriate, rather than impose a sanction, to encourage pupils to reflect on the harmful effects of their misbehaviour.'

The writer of this article does not openly state an opinion. You will have to read between the lines to work out the writer's point of view.

2   Write a summary of this story in two sentences. You could write about:
  • what the government is suggesting
  • what other people think about this.

3   It seems very clear what this news story is about.

  a   Compare the headline and the first sentence of the article. Complete these sentences to explain the difference:
    • The headline says that children will be rewarded if …
    • The first sentence says that children will be rewarded if …

  b   Is the headline wrong, or can you think of another reason why the headline writer might have done this?

4   Do you think the writer of this article thinks that the government's idea is a good one? Write down a quotation from the article that shows this.

Activity 2

1   Look at the caption for the photograph that accompanies the story on page 46.

  a   Why do you think the writer has chosen to describe badly behaved students as 'thugs'?

  b   The writer describes this new campaign as the 'minister's latest bright idea'. What does the phrase 'bright idea' imply? What does the word 'latest' imply?

2   Why has the writer described indiscipline in schools as 'soaring'? What does it imply about behaviour in schools?

3   Count the number of words in the first five paragraphs.

  a   What do you notice about the length of the fifth paragraph?

  b   What effect is the writer aiming to achieve?

  c   How does the word 'absurd' contribute to this effect?

Activity 3

The article on page 46 is about a government campaign for England. Do you think that we should introduce it to Scotland? Will this new idea make students behave better? Will it make good students behave badly? What do you think about whole-class detentions? What would be your policy to improve behaviour?

Write one or two paragraphs expressing your thoughts on improving behaviour in schools.

Activity 4

1   What are the key points the writer makes in the article on page 46? Read the article again and write them in a list. Use the first point on the right to get you started:

Key points

- School students are to be offered rewards to encourage good behaviour.
-
-
-

2   What do you think? For each of the key points you identified in question 1, write a sentence or two in response that expresses your own point of view. You could set them out in a table like the one below. Remember: you may not agree with the example below – you need to express **your own** point of view.

Key points	My point of view
School pupils are to be offered rewards to encourage good behaviour.	Anything that encourages good behaviour in schools must be good.

Activity 5

You are going to use the points of view you wrote down in Activity 4, question 2, to write a letter to the newspaper that published the article on page 46. Respond to the writer's point of view and express your opinion.

To prepare for this task, complete the following.

1   When stating details from the article or the writer's opinion, you can either put them in your own words or use quotations.
    a   Write the following quotation in your own words.
        'Badly behaved youngsters must be praised five times as often as they are punished or criticised.'
    b   Write down a quotation that shows the different rewards pupils will be offered.

2   One way of structuring paragraphs in this kind of writing is to state the writer's opinion and then present your own point of view in response. For example:

The writer suggests that offering rewards for good behaviour is absurd. However, I believe schools should try anything that encourages students to behave well.

Which word shows the link between these two opinions?

3 Once you have added your point of view to the writer's, you can go on to explain it further. Write a sentence that explains the point of view expressed in question 2: why is it so important that students behave well at school?

4 Now that you have explored how to structure and write your paragraphs, you are ready to write your letter. You could use the following structure.

Paragraph 1: introduction
Why are you writing this letter?

Paragraph 2: your first point
The writer's first key point; what you think about it.

Paragraph 3: your second point
The writer's second key point; what you think about it.

Paragraph 4: your third point
The writer's third key point; what you think about it.

Paragraph 5: conclusion
Sum up your opinion and what you think should be done in the future to improve behaviour.

Remember: in paragraphs 2, 3 and 4, you can use the three-part structure you have already practised:
- the writer's opinion
- your opinion
- further explanation of your opinion.

Knowledge about language: Exclamation marks

There are three ways of showing the end of a sentence: a full stop, a question mark or an exclamation mark. The exclamation mark is often used to make writing more like speech: it shows that the writer wants to emphasise a sentence, to say it forcefully as the speech bubbles opposite show.

Stop it!

Be quiet!

Exclamation marks can also suggest a humorous tone. For example:

I like dogs. But I couldn't eat a whole one!

The trouble with exclamation marks is that people sometimes use too many of them. Read the extract called 'My cat!!'. How many of the exclamation marks should be there, and how many would you edit out?

My Cat!!
I love cats! They're so cool! They curl up on your lap and purr and fall asleep! They are the best pets in the world! My cat is called Barbara! Sometimes she catches birds and mice which is so disgusting! But most of the time she is really cute and I love her!

49

8 Bias

You are learning:
- how writers choose language and content to influence the reader's opinion.

Sometimes journalists give both sides of the story – a balanced point of view, the good and the bad, the 'for' and the 'against', the pros and the cons. And sometimes they don't.

Activity 1

Read this article and answer the questions to explore whose side the writer is on – and the content and language used to make the case.

Too much TV may cause attention issues later in life

Young children who watch more than a couple of hours of television a day are more likely to have attention problems as adolescents, researchers have found.

'The two-hour point is very, very clear with our data, very consistent with what the American Academy of Paediatrics recommends,' said study author Carl Erik Landhuis, of the Dunedin School of Medicine at the University of Otago in New Zealand.

'We're not saying don't watch TV, just don't watch too much TV,' he added.

While there is a widespread perception that TV can contribute to attention problems, there is actually very little data on the issue, Mr Landhuis noted in an interview. To investigate, he and his colleagues looked at 1037 boys and girls born in 1972 and 1973, following them from age five to 15.

On average, kids watched about two hours of TV daily when they were five to 11 years old, but were watching 3.13 hours on weekdays by age 13 to 15.

Study participants who had watched more than two hours of TV in early childhood were more likely to have attention problems as young teens, the researchers found. Those who watched more than three hours were at even greater risk. 'Although it doesn't prove causation, it certainly provides evidence that the causal link is in that direction,' Landhuis said.

He and his colleagues suggest that kids who get used to watching lots of attention-grabbing TV may find ordinary life situations – like the classroom – boring. It's also possible, they add, that TV may simply crowd out times spent doing other activities that can build attention and concentration skills, such as reading and playing games.

It's likely, Mr Landhuis said, that kids today watch much more TV than the participants in his study, who had only two channels to choose from in the late 1970s.

From *The Herald*, Saturday, 8 September 2007

1 **a** Do you think that too much TV shortens our attention spans? Answer in two or three sentences.

   b Do you think the writer of this article thinks that too much TV shortens our attention spans? Explain your answer in two or three sentences.

   c Is your opinion the same as the writer's? Has the writer influenced your opinion with his (or her) choice of content and language?

   d Write a sentence explaining why you think the writer has made each of the following choices.

   i – only to quote the researchers.

   ii – to quote a study of 1037 boys and girls over a ten-year period.

   iii – to use words like 'issues' and 'problems'.

   iv – to refer to children as 'kids'.

2 No picture accompanied the story. What kind of picture do you think would be suitable. Describe it.

3 Match the following techniques of biased writing to the examples given in question **1d**.

   a Only one side of the argument is given. The opposition is not given the opportunity to present the other side.

   b Statistics are used to back up the writer's opinion. Sometimes adjectives are added to emphasise the point being made, e.g: 'Lots of attention-grabbing TV …'

   c The writer chooses biased language to emphasise the point.

   d The writer chooses emotive language to exaggerate the point.

   e The writer tries to appeal to the reader's emotions making them feel, for example, sympathy or anger.

Self-evaluation

Create a poster showing some techniques that writers use in biased writing. For each technique, give a definition explaining the technique, and an example. You could use quotations from the article on page 50 as examples, or make them up.

9 Arguing a case

You are learning:
- how to write to argue and persuade.

Writing to argue uses a lot of the same language techniques as biased writing. The purpose of such a text, though, is to change the reader's opinion: to persuade someone that the writer's opinion is the right one.

Activity 1

1 Read this article and think about the writer's point of view.

Are we really becoming more cruel to our pets?

In a week when the RSPCA reported a 77 per cent rise in animal abuse, TREVOR GROVE asks, are we really becoming more cruel to our pets?

The British are known all over the world as a nation of animal lovers, and even mocked for it.

Yet now the RSPCA has come up with dismaying figures to suggest there has been a horrifying rise in cases of cruelty towards our fellow creatures in this country. Last year, the charity went to the aid of almost 100,000 dogs, cats, rabbits, guinea pigs and other animals – an increase of 77 per cent on the previous year.

Among the sickening incidents investigated by RSPCA inspectors was that of a woman who boiled her cat to death in the washing machine.

It must have struggled frantically to escape, as its claws were broken. In another case, a man used an electric carving knife to amputate one of his dog's legs, in order to save the vet's fee.

In 2005, the RSPCA received more than a million calls from worried members of the public. One can only guess at the amount of cruelty and neglect that is actually taking place but never gets reported.

Possibly the RSPCA is right and we have become a bit more careless. But have we really become more deliberately cruel? I suspect quite the opposite.

The very fact that the RSPCA is being besieged by so many reports from concerned members of the public is cause for hope – we are becoming more keenly aware when an animal is being mistreated and we are more eager to report it.

Yes, the growth of rescue organisations for dogs and cats shows that too many stupid, impatient or simply ill-prepared people are sadly prone to abandoning or mistreating pets.

But the very fact such bodies exist and successfully find new homes for thousands of pooches and pussies every year surely suggests a heightened sense of responsibility towards the animals in our midst.

If the RSPCA sees more cases of cruelty towards animals, then that is certainly sad.

But we should not lose sight of the kindness shown towards most species, which is still a distinguishing feature of the British identity.

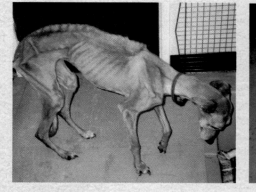

Meg was found starved and neglected; now (pictured right) she has made a full recovery

Daily Mail 27 July 2006

2. What are the key points of this argument? Write a very short summary of each paragraph – then select the three most important key points.

3. Write down one fact from this article. Why do you think the writer included it?

4. Write down one opinion from this article. Why do you think the writer included it?

5. Which of the following techniques that you found in biased writing (pages 50–51) can you spot in this article?
   - statistics
   - emotive language
   - emotional appeal

   Write down an example of each from the text.

6. The writer of this article uses other language techniques to present his argument. Read the definitions of these below, then try to find at least one example of each.

- **Rhetorical questions:** the writer asks the reader a question to involve them in the argument.
- **Examples:** facts or stories used as evidence to prove a point in the argument.
- **A list:** used to emphasise a point.

- **Crushing a counter argument:** the other side of the argument is given, and then shown to be wrong.
- **First person:** 'I' is used to present opinions; 'we' is used to involve and engage the reader in the argument.

Knowledge about language: Apostrophes of possession

Read this sentence: The girl's socks were blue.

The apostrophe plus the 's' mean the girl owns the socks. 'Girl' is the *owner word*. When showing something belonging to someone, the apostrophe goes at the end of the *owner word*, before the 's'.

> Owner + ' + s thing = the thing belongs to its owner.

Write down three more examples using apostrophes to show belonging or possession. Start with this one: The dog's tail.

Things get slightly more complicated when the word is plural. Remember: the apostrophe goes at the end of the owner word; you don't need to add an 's' if the word already ends in 's'.

So if you were writing about two tails belonging to two dogs, or lots of tails belonging to lots of dogs, you would write: The dogs' tails. Now read this:

A boy fell out of a tree. Unfortunately he landed on his friend. I thought that both the boy's arms were broken. It was worse than I thought. Both the boys' arms were broken.

Find the two apostrophes in these sentences. Then explain what happened.

Reading Activity

Close reading

Tuesday 7 November 2006

Take a last look

Photo: Johnathan Hayward/AP

Polar bears play on the tundra near Churchill, Manitoba, Canada, November 2006

They are one of our most beloved animals – but their world is melting away. *Terry Nutkins* on the plight of the polar bear.

Polar bears are one of the most dangerous predators on planet earth. So why do we love them so much? Our fascination goes back a long way. Take Brumas, a polar bear who arrived at London Zoo from the Arctic in the 1940s and in nine years attracted three million visitors. He was a celebrity.

I think we are fascinated with them because they remind us of our childhood – those warm and cuddly toy bears that were with us on dark nights when we couldn't sleep. And as humans, we relate to the way mothers interact with their cubs: teaching them, training them, slapping them, cuddling them. I don't have a problem with anthropomorphism: it's how many people learn about, and love, wildlife.

But the polar bears' world is literally melting away.

For many months of the year, while they are mating and looking after their cubs, the bears do not eat. They simply live off the thick layer of fat that lies beneath their double layer of fur, which keeps out the cold of sometimes –40°C or more. It's when this fat layer runs out that the bears are threatened with dying of starvation unless they can find food quickly.

When the ice forms, the polar bears walk out in search of seals. They need to haul them out of their blow holes and on to the floes to eat. Ten years ago I was filming in the Arctic and saw a lone bear walking on the ice. That was the magic of it: one lone bear walking. They are amazing on the ice, when you consider they can weigh 600 kg to 800 kg and are up to two-and-a-half metres tall. Their feet are covered in fur, which helps them move fast and silently, without slipping.

But global warming is taking its toll. Each year, the ice is later in forming. And since no one is giving the polar bears a weather report in their dens, they have to adapt quickly to this late forming of ice. They might have to wait several weeks before they can get on the ice to find prey – and that is the difference between life and death, certainly for the cubs. To allow these bears to survive – and, of course, many other species – we must as a matter of urgency manage our planet.

The Guardian

Polar bears: fact file

- Polar bears need sea ice to survive.

- Sea ice is shrinking at a rate of 10% every decade.

- Scientists have found polar bears swimming up to 60 miles in open sea.

- Polar bears are starving, cannibalising each other and coming into human areas to scavenge for food.

- In 30 years the Arctic may have no ice in summer.

- By 2040 there will be a significant decline in the numbers of polar bears.

Text for Scotland: Building Excellence in Language

Your task

Read the newspaper article, 'Take a last look' (page 54) and the fact file (page 55), then do the activities below.

1 From paragraph 2 of the article, write down two reasons why people love polar bears.

2 Why do you think the writer has chosen to make paragraph 3 only one sentence long?

3 Using your own words, explain two ways in which polar bears are adapted to live in the Arctic.

4 'So why do we love them so much?' (paragraph 1). What is the effect of the use of 'we' in this question?

5 Write down two examples of geographical language used in this article.

6 Explain how the writer's choice of language suggests that he finds polar bears extraordinary and amazing. In your answer, choose specific words and phrases from the article and comment on them.

7 How does the last paragraph link back to the first?

8 Explain how the layout of this article helps to persuade the reader that people should be concerned about the future of polar bears. In your answer, comment on:

- the choice of headline to get the reader's attention
- how the pictures support the purpose of the article
- the way the article is organised and how this helps to persuade the reader.

3 Gothic tales

Experiences and outcomes

In this unit you will:

Reading
- read a variety of literary texts
- use different reading strategies
- comment on a writer's language choice and craft.

Writing
- use sentences of varying lengths
- use words for precision: adjectives and similies
- use plot development and narrative devices.

Talking and Listening
- collaborate with others
- talk to clarify and so that listeners can follow.

Punctuation and spelling
- use speech punctuation
- look at word endings.

By the end of this unit you will:

- present an audio tour of a haunted house
  Talking and Listening Activity: Drama
- complete a writer's craft piece on a gothic theme
  (Writing Activity: Imaginative writing).

1 Features of Gothic stories

You are learning:
- to recognise the main features of Gothic stories.

Gothic stories became popular around 200 years ago, and have remained popular ever since. Gothic stories and films are usually about ghosts and horror. They often include these features:
- wild and remote places
- dark and gloomy settings
- graveyards, tombs and corpses
- family curses and dark secrets
- supernatural powers
- mysterious and frightening creatures, people or ghosts
- old, ruined, isolated castles and mansions, often with secret passages and mysterious towers
- nightmares, madness and mental torment
- science used for evil or disastrous purposes
- extreme natural events (storms, full moons, etc.).

Activity 1

Look carefully at the list of gothic features above and make a list of stories and films (for example, *Dracula* or *Raven's Gate*) that have some of those features in them.

Activity 2

Read these four story openings.

(A) Shona leaned on the railing of her apartment balcony, gazed across the shiny, blue sea of the bay, and sighed with happiness. This was going to be the perfect holiday. And best of all, there would be no more Ian.

(B) Mirkstane Tower finally rose into view behind a line of dense, gloomy fir trees. The closer we got, the more it looked like a brooding monster – battered and bruised, but still menacing. A fierce wind tugged at its broken shutters.

(C) A sudden dark shadow swept across the bright moon, momentarily blocking out its light. Megan stumbled against a gravestone that was leaning towards the path like a cracked and crooked tooth. An owl gave a ghostly hoot.

(D) 'Surrender!' boomed the voice of the Stragor commander. 'Surrender, or we will destroy your ship and all on board.' Martin Strang, leader of Solar Expedition 29, was not easily scared. He readied the stun missile tubes.

Which **two** of these are most Gothic? Briefly explain why.

Activity 3

Read the extract from *Dr Jekyll and Mr Hyde* by Robert
Louis Stevenson.

The figure haunted Mr Enfield all night; and if at any time
he dozed, it was only to see it glide more stealthily through
sleeping houses, or move the more swiftly through wider
labyrinths of lamp-lighted city, and at every street corner crush
a child and leave her screaming. And still the figure had no face
by which he might know it; even in his dreams it had no face, or
one that baffled him and melted before his eyes; and thus it was
there sprang up and grew apace in his mind a singularly strong,
almost an inordinate curiosity to behold the features of the real
Mr Hyde. If he could but once set eyes on him, he thought the
mystery would lighten and perhaps roll away altogether. He
might see a reason for his friend's strange behaviour and even
for the startling clauses of the will. And at least it would be a
face worth seeing: the face of a man who was without mercy: a
face which had but to show itself to raise up, in the mind of the
unimpressionable Enfield, a spirit of enduring hatred.

Biography

**Robert Louis Stevenson
1850–1894**
Robert Louis Stevenson was
born in Edinburgh in 1850
and studied Law at university,
but his real interests in life
were travelling and writing.
Adventure novels like *Treasure
Island* and *Kidnapped* and
the early horror novel *Dr
Jekyll and Mr Hyde* made him
famous. He has left us with
many pieces of writing that
have become classics.

1 Look again at the list of Gothic features on page 58.
Write down the ones you find in the extract from
Dr Jekyll and Mr Hyde above.

2 Explain how Mr Enfield feels about the 'figure' of Mr Hyde.
Use a table like the one below to explore his feelings.

Word or phrase	What it might show about the narrator's feelings
haunted	Mr Hyde is like a ghost or evil spirit.

3 The passage tells us that Mr Hyde:
 a glides through the street
 b crushes a child and leaves her screaming
 c has no face – at least in Mr Enfield's dream
 d is a 'spirit of enduring hatred'.
 Which, for you, is the most chilling feature of this
 description? Give reasons for your choice.

Self-evaluation

This table shows you how
to get better at the key
reading skills used on
these two pages. How
well are you doing?

Beginner	Competent	Expert
Pick out and describe some basic features of Gothic texts.	Explain how Gothic features are different from those of other sorts of stories.	Consider how the way a text is written affects its meaning.
Comment on how the reader is supposed to feel.	Understand a writer's purpose – even when it is not obvious.	Explain the difference between an author's and a character's viewpoints.

2 Plot

You are learning:
- to understand how a writer structures a story to try to involve the reader.

Stories are all around us. If we listen to a bit of gossip, watch a soap on TV or read a novel, we are enjoying a story. However, written stories need to be well organised to be really interesting. In other words, they need a **plot**.

Activity 1

Think of a TV programme or a film you saw recently – an episode of *Dr Who*, for example. Write down or tell someone what happened, but just give a **summary**.

A good story is far more than just telling someone what happened. It tries to keep us interested. It starts well and makes us want to continue. The telling of the story has to appeal to our curiosity and sense of excitement.

Example: *Dr Who and his assistant land in London some time in the future and they get taken prisoner by …*

Activity 2

When you have finished your summary of what happened, try writing it so that it works as an interesting story. Write the first few lines.

Look carefully at your two versions of 'what happened'. What changes did you have to make to the summary to make it begin to work as a story that someone would want to read?

Example: *When the Doctor was satisfied that the TARDIS had completely settled in its landing place, he pushed open the door and stepped out into the thick, cold mist beyond. 'Mmmmm!' he moaned in delight. 'Delicious fog. Nothing nicer.'*

Activity 3

The story on page 61 is based on a well-known urban legend. An urban legend is a story that has been told so often and by so many people that it starts to sound like a true story. Often these urban legends have an element of horror.

The writer of this version has tried to put the story into a particular order, to build up the reader's interest. The order of the paragraphs gives the story its plot structure.

The story is only five paragraphs long, but the first four paragraphs have been printed in the wrong order, and the last paragraph has been left out entirely.

1 Put the paragraphs in the best order by writing down their letters: A, B, C and D.

Up to scratch

A There was no careful preparation of the body in those days. Corpses were put in coffins and then lowered into the grave as quickly as possible. Funerals were conducted with a haste that we today might think undignified, but at least my great-great-grandmother had a decent, strong wood coffin.

B Even at the graveside my great-great-grandfather sobbed and pleaded for his wife to come back to him. As the rain fell and the first shovelful of soil was thrown onto the lowered coffin, he half jumped, half fell into the grave and draped himself over the coffin lid, hugging it, and begging us to let his wife out. In the end a doctor had to be called to give him a sedative.

C In the night my great-great-grandfather had a terrible nightmare in which he imagined his wife waking up and desperately trying to claw her way out of the coffin. He screamed and flailed his arms around in his tormented sleep, and when the doctor arrived he begged him to have his wife's coffin dug up. The doctor administered another sedative, but my great-great-grandfather was revisited by his nightmare every night that week, and every night he begged the doctor to remove his wife from the grave.

D It is 70 years now since my great-great-grandmother died. She had been ill for some time and her body had wasted away until she was little more than a scarecrow: tatty, dark clothes draped over a stick-thin frame. Her collarbones were as fine and fragile as a bird's. But my great-great-grandfather was devoted to her until the very end, and when she died he was devastated.

E Missing final paragraph.

2 What do you think happens in the missing final paragraph? Write the final paragraph using no more than 100 words.

Knowledge about language: Suffixes

Suffixes are the bits on the ends of words that change or add to those words' meanings. (**Prefixes** do the same job on the *fronts* of words.)

Some common suffixes are: *-ly*, *-ful*, *-ible*, *-able*, *-tion*, *-ment*, *-ic*, *-al*, *-ed*, *-ness*.

1 How many different suffixes can you find in the story 'Up to scratch' above? Give an example of a word with each of these different suffixes.

2 List as many words as you know that end with the suffix *-ness*.

3 Look carefully at the words in your list. Explain what you think *-ness* means.

3 Beginnings and endings

You are learning:
● to make the ending of a story relate to its beginning.

Many writers begin their stories in ways that 'hook' the reader.

Activity 1

1   Read the opening of *Night of the Stick Insects* by Alan Durant, below.

You got any pets? Dog, cat, goldfish maybe? Well, Tommy had lots of pets – jars and tanks of them. Tommy bred stick insects, though I guess it wouldn't be quite right to call them 'pets'. His pet was really the gecko lizard that lived in the big glass tank on his chest-of-drawers. Every now and then he'd get that out and, you know, pet it, stroke it, chat to it, that kind of thing. The stick insects, well they had other uses. Some of them, he sold – and he'd made a fair amount of cash, too. It was amazing how many kids were willing to pay him for the brown stick-like things. At school, there was a craze for them. Tommy thought they were kind of boring himself. They didn't do anything, did they? They just hung about on the wire mesh frame he'd put up against their container wall, imitating twigs. Big deal. He much preferred praying mantises. His dad had a whole collection of those, but he wouldn't let Tommy near them.

2   **a**   How does the writer of *Night of the Stick Insects* try to grab our attention in the opening of the story? He may use a number of ways to do this. Mention at least three different techniques in your answer.
   b   What do you think will happen in the rest of the story?

Activity 2

1   Now read the end of the story, and see if it helps you to decide what has happened.

By the dark, dark early hours of the morning, Tommy's room was thick with stick insects, grown to a gigantic size – some the size of Alsatian dogs. In the blackness they hissed and clicked, as if in angry conversation, discussing what to do. It was to this that Tommy awoke …

His first thought was that he was having another nightmare. And even when they lifted him from his bed with their sturdy, tree-trunk limbs, he could not believe it was real, that this was actually happening. It was only when they lifted him towards the huge, open, slimy, tooth-filled mouth of the now monstrous gecko that he understood the full, real horror of the situation. And by then he was half inside and it was too late.

When we watch a film or read a book, we sometimes find that its mood or tone changes. When speaking, we often convey how we are feeling by tone as well as the words used. Imagine all the possible tones a teacher could use in saying, 'You're late again.' There are many possible moods or tones: happy, tense, humorous, sad, sarcastic and frightening are just some of them.

2 Explain how the tone of the opening is different from the tone of the ending.

   You may like to concentrate on comparing the two short extracts on the right.

Opening
You got any pets? Dog, cat, goldfish maybe? Well, Tommy had lots of pets – jars and tanks of them.

3 Often, clues at the beginning of a story help us to *predict* what will happen at the end.

   a Why do you think the stick insects and the gecko became huge?
   b Explain how clues in the opening of the story prepare us for the ending.

Ending
It was only when they lifted him towards the huge, open, slimy, tooth-filled mouth of the now monstrous gecko that he understood the full, real horror of the situation.

Activity 3

1 Read the opening of a story called *Home*.

You know how it is: new houses have new and unfamiliar noises. 'It's to be expected,' Emily's mother reassured her. But that didn't stop Emily waking up with a gasp every night to the ghostly glow of the moon on the revolting zig-zag patterns of the bedroom carpet. And it didn't mean she stopped worrying about the faint but clear rustling sounds coming from the ancient fireplace – the fireplace that her father had carefully bricked up.

2 What could happen during the story, and how might it end?

3 Write the last 50–100 words of the story.

4 Setting and atmosphere

You are learning:
- how to create an effective setting and atmosphere.

Gothic stories rely heavily on setting and atmosphere. Writers try to create a clear and imaginative setting or 'place' where the action happens. Then they describe that setting in ways that give it a powerful atmosphere or 'mood'.

Biography

Walter Scott (1771–1832) was a Scottish writer and poet who grew up in the Borders, hearing old tales and ballads of supernatural events, which had an important influence on his writing. His novels and poems, often about historical events, were very popular.

Activity 1

Think about a scary film or TV programme you have seen. Think about a particularly frightening part of it. Make a list of the things that helped to terrify you. Typical items might include night (setting); creepy music (atmosphere).

Activity 2

In this extract from *The Bride of Lammermoor* by Sir Walter Scott, the ruined castle of Wolfscrag is described.

1   Read the extract.

Wolfscrag

The pale moon, which had hitherto been [1] with flitting clouds, now shone out and gave them a view of a solitary tower, situated on a [2] cliff, that beetled over the German ocean. On three sides the rock was precipitous; on the fourth, which was that towards land, there was passage for a horseman into the [3] courtyard, encircled on two sides with low offices and stables, partly ruinous. The tower itself occupied one of the remaining sides of the quadrangle. Tall and [4], and built of a greyish stone, it stood glimmering in the moonlight like the sheeted spectre of some huge giant. A wilder, or a more [5] dwelling, it was perhaps difficult to [6].

There was no sign of living inhabitant about this forlorn place, excepting that one, and only one, of the narrow and staunchelled windows which appeared at irregular heights and distances in the walls of the building, showed a small [7] of light.

2   There are seven gaps in the story. Write the numbers 1 to 7 and next to each number write a good word or phrase to fill the gap in the story. Try to choose words that will build the right atmosphere.

Explanations

staunchelled **barred**

3 Look at this *unfinished* sketch of the scene described in *The Bride of Lammermoor*. You will also see a couple of quotations linked to details in the sketch. Copy the sketch, finish it, and then add more quotations from the story.

'The tower itself occupied one of the remaining sides of the quadrangle.'

'On three sides the rock was precipitous …'

Activity 3

Imagine that you are making a film of the extract from *The Bride of Lammermoor*. How would you create a gripping and creepy atmosphere? Use a storyboard like the one below to develop your ideas in detail.

Shot	Sketch of shot	Camera angle	Lighting	Sound	Music
1					
2					
3					

Knowledge about language: Adjectives

Sometimes when we write we use dull, unimaginative words such as *nice*, *big*, *dark*, but to create a creepy atmosphere it is important to choose words more carefully.

Imagine you are walking on a quiet country road. You are on your own and lost. You suddenly come across a large, old, empty-looking house, and you wonder whether to knock and ask for help.

1 Write down at least **ten effective adjectives** to describe the house to make it sound scary. Here are two examples: *gloomy, abandoned*. Now write your own list.

2 When you have done that, try making up **five similes** to describe the house. Here is an example: *like a blind monster*. Now write your own list.

You could use a thesaurus and a dictionary to help you find the best words.

5 Character and suspense

You are learning:
● how a writer creates suspense.

There are many ways in which good writers create suspense or 'tension'. They might:
● describe things in ways that worry us
● make us care about characters so that we worry about them
● make a character sound foolishly unaware of what might be about to happen
● make us expect terrible things are going to happen
● use a variety of sentences to vary the speed of the story (see pages 70–71).

Activity 1

1 Think about the ways in which good writers create suspense as you read this extract from *The Hound of the Baskervilles* by Sir Arthur Conan Doyle. The narrator and Baskerville have very different moods and see things quite differently.

Biography

Arthur Conan Doyle (1859–1930)
Arthur Conan Doyle was a doctor from Edinburgh. He is famous for the many stories he wrote about the detective Sherlock Holmes, who never failed to solve a crime, however complicated.

Baskerville Hall

Over the green squares of the fields and the low curve of a wood there rose in the distance a grey, melancholy hill, with a strange jagged summit, dim and vague in the distance, like some fantastic landscape in a dream. Rolling pasture lands curved upward on either side of us, and old gabled houses peeped out from amid the thick green foliage, but behind the peaceful and sunlit countryside there rose ever, dark against the evening sky, the long, gloomy curve of the moor, broken by the jagged and sinister hills.

At every turn Baskerville gave an exclamation of delight, looking eagerly about him and asking countless questions. To his eyes all seemed beautiful, but to me a tinge of melancholy lay upon the countryside, which bore so clearly the mark of the waning year. Yellow leaves carpeted the lanes and fluttered down upon us as we passed. The rattle of our wheels died away as we drove through drifts of rotting vegetation – sad gifts, as it seemed to me, for Nature to throw before the carriage of the returning heir of the Baskervilles.

Our driver half turned in his seat.

'There's a convict escaped from Princetown, sir. He's been out three days now, and the warders watch every road and every station, but they've had no sight of him yet.'

'Who is he, then?'

'It is Selden, the Notting Hill murderer.'

The road in front of us grew bleaker and wilder over huge russet and olive slopes, sprinkled with giant boulders. Now and then we passed a moorland cottage, walled and roofed with stone, with no creeper to break its harsh outline. Suddenly we looked down into a cuplike depression, patched with stunted oaks and firs which had been twisted bund bent by the fury of years of storm. Two high, narrow towers rose over the trees. The driver pointed with his whip.

'Baskerville Hall,' said he.

Its master had risen and was staring with flushed cheeks and shining eyes. The lodge was a ruin of black granite and bared ribs of rafters.

Through the gateway we passed into the avenue, where the wheels were again hushed amid the leaves, and the old trees shot their branches in a sombre tunnel over our heads. Baskerville shuddered as he looked up the long, dark drive to where the house glimmered like a ghost at the farther end.

2 Using a table like the one below, list all the words and phrases that create a happy, calm atmosphere and all the words and phrases that create a tense, worried atmosphere.

Happy and calm	Tense and worrying
Rolling pasture	Jagged summit

3 Look again at the list of ways writers can create suspense or tension (page 66).

   a Identify five examples of techniques used in *The Hound of the Baskervilles* extract to create suspense and explain how each one suggests that things will turn out badly.
   b In what ways do Baskerville's feelings change during the extract?

Self-evaluation

This table shows you how to improve your story writing.

Beginner	Competent	Expert
• Use description and dialogue to try to build tension.	• Use description and dialogue skilfully and effectively. • Use short sentences to build tension.	• Use description to suggest feelings and atmosphere. • Use sentence structure and punctuation to create tension.

Here is a student's own continuation of the Baskerville Hall passage. What level does it fit? How do you know?

'It's not how I remember it,' said Baskerville, looking worried. We got closer to the house. We could see its dark and dirty windows. Why didn't someone clean them and let the light in? The carriage wheels crunched on the driveway.

6 Dialogue

You are learning:
- how dialogue can make a story more vivid.

Dialogue is the word for people talking to each other in a story or in a play. When characters talk to each other in a soap opera such as *Neighbours* or *Coronation Street,* they are using dialogue. If writers simply described things and summarised for us what characters say, their stories would seem flat and dull. We want to 'hear' the characters speak. The *way* they speak makes them sound real and believable.

Activity 1

Here is a piece of 'reported speech'.

Euan apologised to Shona for not being able to go to the cinema on Saturday because he'd arranged to do something else with his friends. Shona was disappointed and annoyed because it was his idea to go and she'd already bought the tickets.

Now turn it into a piece of dialogue, beginning:
'I'm really sorry,' said Euan, 'but …'

Activity 2

1 You see dialogue in play scripts as well as in stories. Read this play script.

The short way home

Fraser and Emma are walking together.

Fraser: Come on, get a move on. I'm going to be grounded for weeks if I'm late home again. It's all right for you – your parents never seem bothered whether you're out or in.

Emma: Oh chill. We'll get there. But if we head across the cemetery and get through the gap in the hedge, we'll be there in half the time.

Fraser: No chance. I'm not going through the cemetery in the dark. It's freaky. Kirsty McInnes from my bit took a short cut through there and was never seen again.

Emma: Don't be daft. No one knows how Kirsty McInnes disappeared, and no one knows where either. Just because they found her scarf in the cemetery doesn't mean she was ever there.

Fraser: Well you'll never find ME there anyway.

They reach the cemetery. They stop.

Emma: And you'll never find me either. Good night, feartie!

Emma turns and runs into the cemetery.

Fraser: You goon, Emma. Come back. I'm not chasing you, and I'm not waiting on you either. Emma! (*Pause*) I don't like this, Emma. (*Pause*) I'm going.

Emma: (*Calling from some way off*) Come and get me – if you dare.

2 What are the differences between Emma and Fraser's personalities? How does the way they speak show their personalities?

3 Rewrite 'The short way home' as a story instead of a script. (Tip: look below at the rules for speech punctuation.) Start your story like this:

Emma and Fraser walked together down the dark street, Fraser slightly ahead.

'Come on, hurry up!' Fraser pleaded with Emma, 'I'm going to be grounded for weeks if I'm late home again. It's alright for you – your parents never seem bothered if you're out or in.'

Knowledge about language: Speech marks

There are three rules for speech marks:

- Put them at the beginning and end of the words that a character actually speaks.

- Begin the speech with a capital letter and put a punctuation mark inside the end speech marks: a full stop (.), a comma (,), an exclamation mark (!) or a question mark (?).

- Start a new paragraph whenever you change speaker.

Here is some dialogue from a story.

> I can't see you called Fraser Are you over by the gate No Emma replied I'm nearly through the gap in the hedge Where are you

Write out these lines, putting in the correct punctuation and paragraphing.

7 Narrative devices

You are learning:

- to use a range of narrative devices to involve the reader, and to recognise how writers convey setting, character and mood through word choice and sentence structure.

Writers only have words to grab and hold a reader's attention, so it is essential that they choose their words very carefully and design their sentences for maximum effect.

Activity 1

In the following extract from *Raven's Gate* by Anthony Horowitz, Matt is being chased by some ghastly dogs. The writer is trying to create excitement and tension.

1 Read the extract.

Hideous dogs

The first of the creatures had already halved the distance between itself and Matt, yet it didn't seem to be moving fast. It hovered in the air between each bound, barely touching the grass before jumping up again. There was something hideous about the way it ran. A panther or leopard closing in for the kill has a certain majesty. But the dog was deformed, lopsided, ghastly. The flesh on one of its flanks had rotted and a glistening ribcage jutted out. As if to avoid the stench of the wound, the animal had turned away, its head hanging close to its front paws. Strings of saliva trailed from its mouth. And every time its feet hit the ground, its whole body quivered, threatening to collapse in on itself.

Matt reached the fence and clawed at it with his hands, crashing his fingers against the wire. He thought he had run in a straight line, following the way he had come, but he seemed to have got it wrong. He couldn't find the gap. He looked behind him. Two more bounds and the dogs would reach him. There was no doubt that they would tear him apart. He could almost feel their teeth tearing into him, ripping the flesh away from his bones. He had never seen anything so ferocious … not in a zoo, not in a film, not anywhere in the real world.

2 Anthony Horowitz uses a number of techniques to create excitement and tension. Copy and complete this table to explore at least two other ways he does this.

Way of creating tension and excitement	Example	How it works in the extract
Using vivid, unusual words that feed our imaginations.	ghastly	This sounds a bit like 'ghostly' so it is frightening straight away. Also 'ghastly' sounds unhealthy and rather disgusting.
Repeating words and phrases to build up a fast rhythm.		
Using short sentences for impact.		

Writers often end chapters with something that arouses our curiosity and makes us want to read on. This sort of chapter ending is called a **cliff hanger**.

Activity 2

1 Read this extract from near the end of the 'Hideous dogs' chapter of *Raven's Gate*.

2 Below are three possible endings for the chapter. One of them is the ending that Anthony Horowitz actually used. Which version makes the best cliff hanger? Give reasons for your answer.

Matt felt a thump as they drove over the body of one of the dying creatures. But where was the other? He looked around, then yelled out as, still blazing, it slammed into the windscreen, launching itself out of nowhere. For a few seconds it was in front of him, its dreadful teeth centimetres from his face. Then Richard changed into first gear and wrenched the wheel. The dog spun away. Matt looked out of the back window. The flickering remains of one carcass lay in the middle of the road. The second had got snarled up in the wheels, but as the car sped forward it fell free and was tossed to one side.

A They accelerated away, not looking back again. They got home by midnight, and at last they felt safe.

B Richard pulled a face and opened the window. 'So, do you mind telling me what that was all about?' he demanded. Matt didn't know where to begin. 'I think something is happening in Lesser Malling,' he said.
Richard nodded. 'I think you could be right.'

C 'Take that!' Richard yelled as he accelerated off the track and onto the firm road. The car swerved a couple of times before settling down and hurtling into darkness. They didn't speak all the way home. When they got there they parked carefully on the drive and went to bed.

Knowledge about language: Varying sentence structure and length

Here is some very dull writing. How could you vary the sentences to make them more interesting to read?

There was moonlight. The curtains were open. I saw a woman. She was lying still on the bed. She was wearing a white robe. A demon was sitting on her. I was scared.

Rewrite these lines to make them exciting and full of tension. Don't invent any new details; just improve the style.

8 Developing character

You are learning:
- to appreciate how a writer creates expectations in a reader and gets them interested in characters.

On page 58 you learned about the typical features of Gothic stories. When we come across these features in a story, we expect that it will involve ghosts or horror.

Activity 1

1   Read the opening of *The Drowning Pond* by Catherine Forde.

> So.
>   It *did* end up here.
>   Merlock Country Park on Hallowe'en night.
>   According to Isabella there was even supposed to be a full moon.
>   'Imagine. A witch's moon for us, Nicky. Perfect eh?' Isabella hissed in my ear while we scrambled the low dyke, sneaking into the park.

2   Make a list of the words or phrases in this opening that suggest *The Drowning Pond* is going to be a ghost or horror story. Explain each of your choices in a table like the one on the right.

Words	Explanation	
hissed in my ear	The word 'hissed' suggests a sinister and evil tone. 'In my ear' suggests secret plots.	

Activity 2

If we become interested in characters, then we start to care about them, and the writer can make us want to know what is going to happen to them.

1   Read how the opening of *The Drowning Pond* continues.

'You're not here to like it, are you, stupid?'
   Don't ask me how Isabella could have heard us talking, what with the rain rattling and the wind whistling out of tune to make the branches dance. Soon as Margaret spoke, however, Isabella swung her light into Margaret's face, whipping the skirts of her ankle length black mac after. I'm not kidding, in that get-up she made a perfect stunt double for the Wicked Stepmother in Snow White: cascading dark hair, glittering eyes, red lips. Beautiful. Cruel. She even blooming cackled like her, 'We've made it! Hallowe'en at the Drowning Pond. Let's drink to that.'

2 What can we work out about Isabella's personality from this paragraph?

Here are some words that *might* be used to describe Isabella:

stupid   unkind   a bully   creepy   bossy

glamorous   amusing   odd   boastful   disgusting

a Which **two** words in the list **best** describe Isabella?
b Explain why you have chosen each of those words.
c Which word is **least** true of Isabella? Why?
d Use two of **your own words** to describe what Isabella is like.
e How might the story continue? Try to write the next five lines.

Activity 3

1 Read how Catherine Forde introduces another character.

> I mean Lizzie was pale, really pale now with all her hair shaved, but her eyes, fringed by dark, dark lashes, seemed huge. They flashed green and smiley at Alan and Old Groat, her stare direct. Confident like I could never be.

2 a What can you tell about Lizzie from this description? Why?
b What can you tell about the narrator (Nicky) from this?

Knowledge about language: Commas

Commas have many uses. These include:
- separating items in a list
- parenthesis – where extra information is added and separated from the rest of the sentence by a pair of commas.

Look at the commas that Catherine Forde uses in the extracts from *The Drowning Pond*.
1 Find an example where commas are used to separate items in a list and write it down.
2 Find an example where a pair of commas is used to add extra information and write it down. Explain what the extra information is about.

9 Attention to detail

You are learning:
- to involve a reader by using a lot of imaginative detail.

Good stories usually have a lot of rich detail that stirs up the readers' imagination, allowing them to 'see' a scene in their head.

Activity 1

Many of the early Gothic writers were fascinated and inspired by Henry Fuseli's 1781 painting *The Nightmare*. Look carefully at the painting. What do you see?

1   For each character (the woman, the dwarf and the horse) write down three details. Try to be very factual, for example, 'The woman's left arm is dangling over the bed with the knuckles just touching the floor.'

2   Now write down possible explanations for what you see. For example, 'The woman might be limp because she is dead, deeply asleep or drugged.'

Self-evaluation

You have tried to notice all the detail in the painting and make sense of it. Some students were asked to 'write the painting' as though it were a scene from a story. Here are the criteria the students used to help them improve their writing:

Beginner	Competent	Expert
• Use adjectives and adverbs. • Use a mixture of long and short sentences.	• Use adjectives, adverbs, similes and metaphors. • Use a mixture of long and short sentences, which begin in different ways.	• Use well-chosen adjectives, adverbs, similes and metaphors. • Vary the structure of your sentences to create the atmosphere you want.

Here is part of one student's version of the painting-as-a-story. This is a 'beginner' level piece of writing.

As I entered the room the moon came out from behind the clouds and flooded the room with a pale, white light. Sarah was lying on the table. She was stretched out, wearing a long, white robe. My heart thumped because she looked dead. Her head was hanging over the edge of the table and one arm was dangling down to the floor.

Look back at the criteria. What level would you give to this second version? Why?

In the moonlight coming from the open window, Jane was draped over the bed in the centre of the room. I knew I was too late: although she was robed in a beautiful white gown, and her head and arm hung peacefully over the table's edge, blood had soaked into her outer robe, and her face and neck had a corpse-like paleness. And on her body sat a mean and triumphant demon, his grinning shadow printed grimly on the red curtains behind.

Now try writing your own version of the painting. Make sure you use the criteria to guide you in making your writing as good as possible.

10 Language for effect

Writers – and speakers – always have to choose their words carefully. This is true of non-fiction as well as stories. Being careful means thinking hard about:
- *what* you are trying to achieve
- *who* your audience (or reader) is.

For instance, if you want to give *information* to a group of ten-year-olds, you would choose simple, straightforward language and you could use some slang words. On the other hand, if you wanted to *persuade* your headteacher to reduce your homework, you would have to choose words and a style that were much more formal.

Activity 1

A tourist attraction called Nightmare Closes has recently opened in Edinburgh. Visitors explore life-size models of old buildings and streets where terrible crimes and accidents have taken place, and which are widely believed to be haunted.

1 Read this leaflet, designed to persuade people to visit Nightmare Closes.

Nightmare Closes

Dusk gropes its way stealthily through the tightly packed closes and back courts of old Edinburgh, filling its inhabitants with dread and scattering them to seek shelter in their cramped and poorly-lit homes. As darkness tightens its grip on the city's slums, sinister shadows slip around corners and lie in wait for their prey. The city's deathly secrets, so long shut up in these grim walls, are stirring and returning to haunt their old hideouts: the silhouette of a well-dressed gentleman sharpens his knife and blends patiently into a broken stairmouth. Sinister and cruel threats whisper around the closes. A sudden scream pierces the eerie quiet.

The only people who dare remain in these grim streets are the insane, the foolish, the homeless – and **you**.

Edinburgh's newest and spookiest attraction is open for business. Come and explore the **Nightmare Closes** of old Edinburgh. Thrill to the authentic sounds, sights and smells of the city's close-packed slums. Be haunted by the ghosts of Burke and Hare, who, when they could not dig up enough dead bodies to satisfy the dissection rooms of the medical school, turned to murder. Feel the hairs rise on your neck as you step across the mass graves of the plague dead.

You never know what is waiting for you round the next corner. Come and find out – if you dare!

2 The writer uses a number of ways to persuade us to visit Nightmare Closes. For example, she uses the present tense to make us feel as if we are already there, and she uses unusual and threatening words.

   a Find and write down an example of:
- the present tense
- threatening words.

   b Write down and explain at least two other ways the writer uses to make us want to visit Nightmare Closes.

Activity 2

The owners of Nightmare Closes decided to publicise the attraction in a number of ways in order to appeal to different types of people. Here is part of a radio advert aimed at Edinburgh teenagers.

Radio advert script

Sound of creaking door echoing.

Michelle: Oooooh, I don't like this. It's pitch black in here and dead freaky.

Darren: You go first. Unless you're feart?

Michelle: I'm no feart. It totally freaks me out though. Gie's yer haun. 'Mon, let's go.

Spooky music, building up. Shuffling footsteps. Whispering voices. Sudden silence.

Michelle: Darren? Whit ye daein'? Whit's happened tae yer haun? It's a' scaly like. Darren? *She screams suddenly*

Voice over: Nightmare Closes. Edinbugh's newest and spookiest attraction. Just five minutes from Edinburgh Castle. But years back in time. It's *so* not boring.

Michelle: *(Nervously)* Darren? Yer haun's here but whaur's the rest o' ye?

Voice over: Nightmare Closes. Open all year round. ... [*slogan missed out*]

1 Explain how this advert tries to appeal to young people.

2 The final slogan has been missed out of the script. Here are three possible slogans:
   a Visit us soon.
   b Your worst nightmare ... and some.
   c It's spooky.
   Which do you think is the best slogan, and which is the worst? Why?

3 Think up a better slogan of your own. Explain why it is a good slogan.

4 If possible, work with a group of students to act out and record the Nightmare Closes radio advert, finishing with the best slogan.

Talking and Listening Activity

Drama

Welcome to Murder Castle!

You are now going to prepare a Talking and Listening task in a group. This is one of your main assessments in this Gothic unit.

Your task

You are the publicity team for Murder Castle, a medieval tower house that is open to the public. You have been asked to prepare commentary about the castle for visitors to listen to on headphones.

Preparing for your Talking and Listening Activity

There are two parts to this assessment:
- group planning
- group presentation.

You need to make sure you get along with the other members of your group and that you help each other to work successfully.

1 Look carefully at the layout of Murder Castle and agree the best route through the building.

2 Agree a role for each member of your group.

Chairperson
You are responsible for leading the discussion. You must make sure everyone has their say and the task gets done.

Scribe
You are responsible for making a note of every decision that is taken by the group.

Other members of the group
You are responsible for taking an active part in the discussion, listening to others and following the instructions of the chairperson.

3 Look together at the success criteria for group planning.

Beginner	Competent	Expert	How to do it
• Listen carefully. • Contribute ideas and justify them. • Ask questions about other people's ideas and views.	• Listen and show that you are listening. • Make contributions that take account of others' views, showing sensitivity and understanding towards them. • Ask questions to develop ideas.	• Take an active part in discussion. • Develop others' contributions and come up with compromises that others can accept. • Show sensitivity and understanding towards others' ideas.	• Make some notes; nod; say things like 'OK', 'I see'. • Only speak when you have something good to say. Make your views clear. • Be polite. Be patient. Show respect for other people's ideas and feelings. • Make decisions efficiently. Don't waste time.

4 • As a group, plan your commentary recording so that it will meet at least the competent criteria.

   • Discuss in detail how you will have to talk, listen and behave to meet those criteria. Use the 'How to do it' column above as a starting point for your discussion.

   • Keep referring back to the criteria as you work together, and talk about the progress you are making.

5 Decide which rooms or parts of the castle your group is going to cover (your group could include some of its own ideas here).

6 • Decide what you are going to say about each room or part of the castle.

   • Agree who is going to present the commentary for each room or part of the castle. Each person should then make some notes about what they are going to say (remember you should not write out every word).

7 Practise giving your commentary for each room in turn, remembering to make it interesting for your listeners.

11 Writer's craft

You are learning:
● to show you understand writer's craft by continuing a story in the same style as it began.

It's almost impossible to write out a story that's perfect first time; the best stories are planned and developed in meticulous detail.

Activity 1

1 Read the following extract from *Whispers in the Graveyard* by Theresa Breslin.

I'm running. My chest is tight and sore. Breath rasping and whistling in my lungs. Branches whip against my face. Brambles tear at my legs and arms. There is a voice screaming. Out loud. The sound ripping through the trees, screaming and screaming.

It's my voice.

'Amy! Amy!'

Now I'm at the back dyke and the solid wooden fencing has been torn aside. Blasted apart as if some careless giant had passed by and trodden on it. I stare at the wood, not splintered or broken, but melted. Dissolved and warped. Curled aside to make a small space. Space enough for a child to walk through. What could do that? What power is there that would leave that mark?

I hesitate, feeling the first great lurch of fear for myself.

'Amy?' I cry out.

Beyond me the gaping dark of the cemetery.

There is a soft shudder in my head. A strange flicker which fastens on my fear. Nothing calling for me this time. No whispers in my face tonight.

Why?

Because Amy is in there. With one child captive, there is no need for two.

2 Use a table like the one below to identify WHO is involved. Decide whether they are friends or related in some way.

Character	Age? Boy or girl?
Amy	
'I'	

3 There are various clues that some supernatural power is at work, as these examples show.

'I stare at the wood, not splintered or broken, but melted.'
'What power is there that would leave that mark?'
'No whispers in my face tonight.'

Activity 2

The extract on page 80 is written in the present tense. Look opposite to how it would be written in the past tense. What difference does writing in the present tense make?

> I was running. My chest was tight and sore. Breath was rasping and whistling in my lungs. Branches whipped against my face. Brambles tore at my legs and arms. There was a voice screaming.

Activity 3

In the extract on page 80, the writer uses a number of minor sentences, which do not have a finite verb. If they were rewritten as 'proper' sentences they would look like this.

> There is a voice screaming out loud. The sound rips through the trees, screaming and screaming.

In the paragraph beginning 'Now I'm at the back dyke …' there are four minor sentences. Identify them and rewrite them as proper sentences with finite verbs. Look at your rewrite and compare it to the original. What effect do the minor sentences have?

Self-evaluation

1 Look back through everything you have done in this unit. Make a list of the most important things you have learned about writing stories in the gothic genre.

2 Write down three things that you will you need to do to make this writer's craft piece the best you have ever written. Remember to use the criteria on page 75.

Writing activity

Imaginative writing

Whispers in the Graveyard

Your task

Continue the story that starts on page 80.

- Remember to use the first person (I and me) and the present tense.
- Keep the same characters (Amy and the narrator) although you can introduce new ones.
- Keep the same setting (the graveyard with the broken fence, surrounded by woods).

You should include the following:

- some features of horror stories
- carefully chosen words and phrases to build up a spooky, scary atmosphere
- some minor sentences to give dramatic impact to the narrator's thoughts.

You could begin your first chapter:

> As I emerged from the brambles, I could see the ghostly
> outline of the gravestones against the pale light of the moon ...

Tick list of features

Use the tick list below to check you have included some of the relevant features that your story is going to be assessed on.

Tick list of features	✓ I have included this
Carefully chosen words and phrases to create a: ● spooky setting ● mysterious supernatural element ● sense of tension.	
A variety of sentences: ● short sentences and minor sentences to increase tension ● longer sentences elsewhere ● start sentences in different ways. ● use a variety of connectives.	
A range of punctuation: ● capital letters, question marks and full stops ● commas ● punctuation of speech.	

Remember to check your work carefully before you hand it in!

4 Our world

WOOF!

QUEEN

'A HUGE SUGAR-RU[...]
OF ENERGY' SCOTSM[...]

Alan Bissett

Experiences and outcomes

In this unit you will:

Reading

- read texts around the theme of Scotland's cultures
- identify the main ideas in a text
- comment on a writer's language choice and craft.

Writing

- organise sentences within a paragraph
- organise ideas in a sequence of paragraphs
- use imagery in your writing.

Words and sentences

- revise the elements in a simple sentence
- expand the range of linking words and phrases you use (connectives).

By the end of this unit you will:

- read a range of texts by Scottish writers on Scottish cultures and identities (Close reading)
- write about your own local area and culture (Functional writing).

1 Cultures of Scotland

English, Scots and Gaelic are the three main languages spoken in Scotland today. This unit looks at the Scots language and Scottish identity through a variety of texts.

Scottish Standard English is very similar to the Standard English spoken throughout the UK. However, there are many expressions used in Scotland which would either not make sense or be surprising to people from elsewhere in the UK.

Activity 1

Match each Scottish Standard English expression to its meaning in Standard English .

Scottish Standard English	Standard English
I need to get some messages.	I'll take you home.
I have a sore pinkie.	They won't come.
The kettle needs filled.	I live in Edinburgh.
I stay in Edinburgh.	I have some shopping to do.
Special uplifts.	The kettle needs filling.
I'll get you home.	My little finger hurts.
They'll not come.	Special collections.

Six hundred years ago, many languages could be heard in Scotland. In the Northern Isles of Orkney and Shetland, Norn was spoken – a language with roots in Scandinavia. In the Western Isles and throughout the Highlands, Gaelic was spoken, much more widely than it is today. The Scottish Church used Latin and many Scottish nobles spoke French. The language used by the King and his government was known as 'Inglis'. It was what we would now call Scots, with distinctive grammar and vocabulary.

Scottish church used Latin

Many Scottish nobles spoke French

NORN

GAELIC

INGLIS

Activity 2

Traces of these languages can still be seen today in the names of places. Look at these Norn, Gaelic and Old English words which are still used in place names of today.

Norn	Gaelic	Old English
ness = headland	strath = valley	burgh = town
wick = bay	auch = field	aber = river mouth
kirk = church	ben = mountain	
	kin = head, summit	
	kil = church	

1   Make a list of place names from your local area or from elsewhere in Scotland that include each of these: Norn, Gaelic and Old English.

2   Read the extract below from Alan Bissett's novel *The Incredible Adam Spark*. It is easier to understand if you read it aloud.

That's me man: he-man! Ken how cos it's the hallglen and glen village gala day man – yahoo! – the gala days the best day of the year man, always sunny roastin boilin boof ge the t-shirt off dudes! Aye. Everybodys dead xcited. Big prade oom-pa-pa oom-pa-pa, we all march marchtay the big grass park nextay the cottages barandlounge and there's a corry-na-shin by a slebrity who says i now pronounce you the hallglen and glen village gala day queen. And sometimes? Ooh. The slebritys a local deejay or the member of parlymint for falkirk west or kelly marie! Off tvs river city. Whoaaah kelly marie from river city? And the queen well she touches her crown and says in a weepolitevoice as queen i promise to help all the good people of hallglen, and the good people of hallglen they all cheer. Raay! Theres a fancy dress prize, And im he-man!

1   List three words which are not Scots words but which the writer has chosen to spell differently. Write their Standard English spellings beside them.

2   List all the Scots words and expressions you can find in this text.

3   Write another three sentences about a gala day in the same style as this extract, using Scots words and expressions that you know.

2 Scots Language in the north east

You are learning:
- to understand the Scots language of the north east (Doric).

The north east of Scotland has a strong tradition of 'bothy ballads'. These poems, rooted in farming life, are generally humorous and have a rich variety of Scots words and expressions from this area.

Activity 1

Opposite are some verses from a song in Scots about the adventures of a drunken pig. Below is an English summary of what happens in each verse, but in the wrong order.

1 Match each verse to the English summary below.

(A) They had various kitchen utensils and planned to give the pig a good beating, but the pig was so drunk by then that it made no difference.

(B) They all ran screeching to the door but it was stuck. McGinty shouted for an axe – he wasn't going to be locked out of any room in his own house.

(C) Johnny Murphy was jumping over the pig when he tripped on a dish full of dripping, fell down, hit his head and burst into tears.

(D) McGinty's pig had got into the house and headed for the storeroom where he found a barrel of whisky and started to drink it. He liked it very much.

(E) The pig was so drunk he could hardly stand. McGinty and his foreman had to carry him out of the house on a shutter.

(F) And the pantry shelf came down and he was lying moaning with all sorts of sticky food on top of him. He got no sympathy from Mrs McGinty, who only cared about the state of the floor.

(G) Mrs McGinty was going through to the kitchen in the dark when she fell head over heels over the pig which she was not expecting to be there.

(H) They got an axe, chopped through the door and it sprang open. They shot through to the next room like potatoes rumbling out of a bucket.

Activity 2

Work out the meanings of the words from the poem (in the boxes opposite) and write the definitions. If you get stuck, the summary of the poem in English will help.

toddy   greetin'

heelster gowdy   ashet

girnin'   skirlin'

rummelin'

tatties

McGinty's Meal and Ale

1 Noo McGinty's pig had broken lowse an' wannert tae the lobby
Whaur he open shived the pantry door an' cam' upon the toddy;
An' he took kindly tae the stuff, like ony human body,
At McGinty's meal and ale, whaur the pig ga'ed on the spree.

2 Miss' McGinty she ran but the hoose, th' way was dark an' crookit.
She ga'ed heelster gowdy ower the pig, for it she never lookit,
And she lat oot a skirl, wid've paralysed a teuchit,
At McGinty's meal and ale, whaur the pig ga'ed on the spree.

3 Johnny Murphy he ran efter her and ower the pig wis leapin',
When he trampit on an ashet that was sittin' fu' o' dreepin'.
An' he fell doon and peel't his croon an' couldnae haud frae greetin',
At McGinty's meal and ale, whaur the pig ga'ed on the spree.

4 And the pantry shelf cam' rattlin' doon an' he was lying kirnin',
Amang saft soap, paysmeal, cornflour an' yirnin'
Like a golloch amang treacle, but McGinty's wife was girnin'
At the sotter on her pantry flair, an' widnae let him be.

5 Sine they a' ran skirlin' tae the door, but foun' that it wis tuggit,
For aye it held the faister, aye the mair they ruggit,
Till McGinty roared tae bring an axe, he widnae be humbuggit –
Nae, nor lockit in his ain hoose, an' that he'd let them see.

6 Sine the wife cam' trailin' wi' an axe, an' through the bar was hackit
An' open flew the door at aince, sae ticht as they was packit,
An' a' the crowd came rummelin' out, like tatties frae a bucket
At McGinty's meal and ale, whaur the pig ga'ed on the spree.

7 They had spirtles, they had tatty chappers, faith they werenae jokin',
An' they swore they'd gar the pig claur whaur he wis never yokin'
But by this time the pig was fu' and didnae care for talkin',
At McGinty's meal and ale, whaur the pig ga'ed on the spree.

8. Oh there's eely pigs and jeely pigs an' pigs for haudin' butter
Aye, but this pig was greetin' fu' an rowlin' in the gutter,
Till McGinty an' his foreman trailed him oot upon a shutter
Frae McGinty's meal and ale, whaur the pig ga'ed on the spree.

3 Shetlandic Scots

You are learning:

● to recognise and appreciate Shetlandic Scots language.

Shetland is the most northerly group of islands in Scotland. The Scots spoken here has influences from Scandinavia.

Biography

Christine De Luca is a Shetlander, living in Edinburgh. She writes both in English and Shetlandic, her mother tongue. Her first two poetry collections won the Shetland Literary Prize.

Activity 1

1 Read the poem below written in Shetlandic by Christine De Luca and her translation of it into English.

Ice Floe on-line

We scrit wir wirds ta mak connection
wi laands whaar eence der wir a link;
dan send dem dirlin alang meridians
tae aa erts aroond wir virtual wirld.

Eence uncans cam bi oar or sail:
a lang sea circle vaege, da wirds
maist likely faered. Wir wirds birl
aff a satellites an starns; loup an tirl,

crackle lik mirry-dancers i da lift.
We set dem sheeksin owre Arctic distances
ta gently rummel Babel's To'er, an bigg
instead a hoose ta hadd wir difference.

Ice Floe online

We write our words to make connection
with lands where once there was a link;
then send them zinging along meridians
in all directions round our virtual world.

At one time news came by oar or sail:
a long sea circle journey, the words
most likely feared. Our words dance
off satellites and stars; they leap and twirl,

crackle like aurora borealis in the sky.
We set them blethering across arctic distances
to gently topple Babel's Tower, and build
a house instead to hold our difference.

2 Using the translation, write a glossary for the Shetlandic version, explaining the following words:

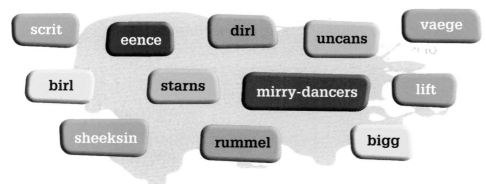

scrit eence dirl uncans vaege
birl starns mirry-dancers lift
sheeksin rummel bigg

Activity 2

1 How did news travel in the olden days according to this poem?

2 Which of the following modern means of communication do you think de Luca was thinking of when she wrote 'Ice-floe online'?
   - email
   - telephone
   - msn messenger
   - letters
   - postcards?
   Give reasons for your choices.

3 List all the positive words De Luca uses as she writes about modern communication.

4 Choose the line you like best from the Shetlandic version and write it down. Explain why you like it – is it because of the words, sound, ideas or something else?

5 Choose the line you like best from the English translation and write it down. Explain why you like it.

Self-evaluation

How skilled are you in explaining why you like a particular line or extract? Mark your answers to questions 4 and 5 according to the following criteria.

Beginner	Competent	Expert
Can explain preference giving simple reason.	Can explain preference clearly, commenting on word choice/ sound/ideas in detail.	Can explain preference clearly, with insightful and detailed comment on word choice/sound/ideas.

4 Identifying main ideas

You are learning:
- to select relevant evidence from a text.

When you write about a text, you need evidence to support your ideas and opinions. You can use phrases or sentences from the text to do this.

Activity 1

1 Read this extract from *Growing up in the Gorbals* by Ralph Glasser. The writer was the son of Jewish immigrants from Lithuania who arrived in Glasgow a few years after he was born.

Biography

Ralph Glasser (1916–2002) grew up in Glasgow, the son of Lithuanian Jewish parents. He won a scholarship to Oxford and became an economist. He worked for the British Council and later became an advisor to various African and Asian governments.

RALPH GLASSER

GROWING UP IN THE GORBALS

Boy at Oxford, Gorbal Voices, Siren Songs

THREE BOOKS IN ONE VOLUME

When I was about nine, I challenged a boy who was kicking me in class; we would fight in the playground after school. I was short-sighted and wore glasses, and soon, in the gathering gloom of the winter afternoon, with the tight circle of boys – none of them Jews – around us, I was getting steadily beaten up. I went on slugging it out, or tried to, for my opponent was much stronger and a much better boxer. After a time my glasses fell off and my nose bled.

'Are ye gointae gie' up?' he shouted.

Something made me shout back: 'Not till ye say ye're sorry!'

He stopped in amazement: 'Whit for?'

'For callin' me a Sheeny.'

'But ye are a Sheeny, aren't ye?'

We started fighting again. A few moments later, when I thought I could not stand up much longer, an older boy shouted from the crowd: 'Hey, it's no' fair, he's gettin' beat. Come on. Stop it.'

The crowd filtered away. Someone had picked up my glasses and now gave them to me and wandered off.

I was never attacked again. That perhaps proves nothing. But it must be remembered that part of the prejudice of the time was that the Jew was somehow slippery, hard to pin down, a coward. I had stood and fought, and though I had lost the battle, I had done something to weaken the myth.

When I got home, father spoke more in sadness than to chide me: 'Don't get into trouble again. Always remember, if a Jew gets into trouble he's always blamed more than the Goy [non-Jew]. It's the way the world is.'

a Why was Ralph angry with the boy he was fighting?

b What ended the fight?

c What did Ralph's father think about the fact that Ralph had been fighting?

Activity 2

Look again at the extract on page 90 and decide whether you agree or disagree with each of the statements below. Find evidence from the extract to support your answer.

	Agree or disagree	Evidence
1 Ralph won the fight.		
2 Ralph was right to fight the bully.		
3 Some of those watching the fight supported Ralph.		
4 Ralph's father was angry that his son had been fighting.		

Knowledge about language: Parts of a sentence

The brothers ate their dinner.

subject   verb   object

1 In the sentences below, circle the verbs and underline and label the subject and object.
   • A boy at the school bullied Ralph for being Jewish.
   • Ralph fought the boy who had picked on him.

2 Write two simple sentences with Ralph as the subject of the sentence and someone else as the object. Underline and label the subject and object in each sentence.

Explanations

subject tells us who or what a sentence is about
verb tells us what a person or thing does
object tells us who or what has been affected by what was done

5 Narrative techniques

You are learning:
- the difference between first person and third person narrative and why authors choose a particular narrative technique.

Writers make choices about who tells a story.
- In a first-person narrative, a character who is part of the story uses 'I' and 'we' to tell the story. This allows the reader to see what the character is thinking and feeling from their perspective.
- In a third-person narrative, the story is told by someone outside the story using 'he', 'she' and 'they'.

Activity 1

Look again at the extract from *Growing up in the Gorbals* on page 90.

1 Does Glasser use the first person or third person narrative? Quote a line from the extract to support your choice.

2 Why do you think Glasser chooses this narrative technique for *Growing up in the Gorbals*?

3 Ralph's father speaks differently from Ralph. Explain as fully as you can what the differences are.

4 Why do you think there are these differences? (Clue: Look at the introduction to the text.)

Activity 2

Read the following extract from *Divided City* by Theresa Breslin.

Biography

Theresa Breslin is an author of young adult fiction. She began writing when working as a librarian. She was born and brought up in a small town in the middle of Scotland close to castles, old burial grounds and the Roman Wall, all of which helped fuel her imagination.

'It really gets to me the way some people feel free to make remarks about the size of your family and actually believe you might sympathize with child-murdering terrorists,' Joe had heard his Aunt Kathleen ranting on to his father one day. 'In the shop even, by my own customers, I'm told what my opinion is on certain things. Every time Celtic has a win I get: "You'll have been celebrating the other night, eh?" I can't stand football, and my Tommy supports Partick Thistle. Many's the time I've felt like letting the hot tongs slip against a bare neck.'

'Let them say what they like,' Joe's granny chipped in. 'It's what they used to do that was worse. Open discrimination. It's not so long ago that building sites had signs up: NO IRISH NEED APPLY. The London Times carried adverts for maids that said: NO CATHOLICS.'

'Those days are gone, Mother,' Joe had heard his dad say. 'We shouldn't live in the past.'

'It's all very well for you to say that, Joseph. Remember, it wasn't my past. It was my present.'

'It's the past now,' his dad insisted.

'Is it?' his mother asked.

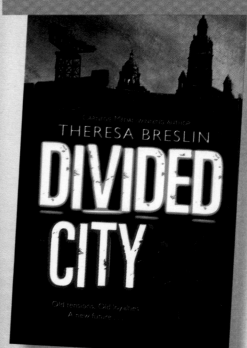

THERESA BRESLIN

DIVIDED CITY

Activity 3

Look again at the extract from *Divided City*.

1 Write down two ways in which Irish immigrants were discriminated against in the past.

2 What makes Aunt Kathleen angry with her customers?

3 Does Joe's father believe that Catholics are discriminated against today? Give evidence from the extract to support your answer.

4 Does Joe's granny believe that Catholics are discriminated against today? Give evidence from the extract to support your answer.

Activity 4

1 *Divided City* is a novel, so the author could have chosen to use first person or third person narrative. Look at the extract on page 92 again and then read the extract below. Why did the author decide to tell the story using the third person narrative?

> 'I need a minute.' Joe stepped off the street into an ornate doorway.
> 'Hang on,' said Graham, as he took in the sign outside:
> ST FRANCISCUS CATHOLIC CHURCH
> 'I'm not going in there.' He grabbed Joe's arm. 'What are you up to?'
> 'Are you scared to come inside?' Joe challenged him.
> 'No,' said Graham. He followed Joe into the interior of the building and hung back at the door as Joe went over to a stand of candles. A man who might be a priest came walking up the main aisle. Supposing this man said something to him? He wouldn't know how to answer. Weren't you supposed to call them 'Father' or something? No way could he do that. And what if the man asked him a question? He'd know straight away that Graham wasn't a Catholic.

2 Write out the first sentence of the first extract from Joe's point of view changing 'Joe' to 'I' and making any other changes necessary.

3 Write out the last sentence of the second extract from Graham's point of view.

I followed Joe into the interior of the building...

Self-evaluation

Choose the traffic light that shows how confident you are at recognising and writing in the first person.

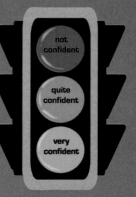

not confident
quite confident
very confident

93

6 Organising ideas

You are learning:
● to organise ideas in a sequence of paragraphs

The first sentence of a paragraph is called the topic sentence. The topic sentence explains what the paragraph will be about, rather than specific details.

Activity 1

1   On pages 90-93 you read about two different groups who came to Scotland to settle – Jews from Eastern Europe and Roman Catholics from Ireland. Read the passage below about the arrival of Indians and Pakistanis to Scotland.

India had been part of the British Empire for many years but British rule came to an end in 1947. At that time, a separate state was set up for Indian Muslims known as Pakistan. In the 1950s, as British businesses struggled to find workers to fill jobs, people from countries which had recently been part of the Empire were encouraged to come and work here. Pakistanis came to work in the jute mills of Dundee. Glasgow employed Indians and Pakistanis to work on buses and trams.

But many new arrivals faced racism and were unable to find jobs. So they set up their own small shops and businesses, working long hours. In the 1970s, Asians who had settled in Uganda (in Africa) fled to Britain to avoid persecution when the dictator Idi Amin came to power. Many of them also set up small businesses.

2   Imagine you are planning to write a short account on immigration to Scotland. Consider the list of possible topics on the right. What would be the best order to place them in?

3   Write a topic sentence to begin a paragraph on each of the topics opposite.

(A) What is immigration? Something to get the reader interested in this issue.

(B) How different groups were affected by prejudice and racism.

(C) Examples of different groups which have immigrated to Scotland.

(D) Examples of books which tell of their experiences.

(E) Different reasons for immigrating to Scotland (work, avoiding persecution)

Activity 2

Use the planning you have done in Activity 1 write a short account of immigration to Scotland. Use the information from pages 90–94.

Reading Activity
Close reading

From Greenland to Scotland

The following extract comes from *Fallen Pieces of the Moon* by Robin Lloyd Jones. It is about a sea-kayaking trip to Greenland.

1   We hauled out on a sloping slab of rock, the only possible landing place for miles, which bore long furrows as if a giant tiger had raked it with its claws. The main Ice Age, which had scoured this land like a giant file 8–12000 years ago, had picked the landscape clean, leaving only the Earth's ancient, bare bones. All around, steep, dark-blue mountains ringed a slate sea, which made the icebergs seem all the whiter. I had been told I'd find this part of Greenland in July like the Scottish hills in March. If I ignored the icebergs and the fact that everything was bigger and steeper, I could see a vague likeness. There were large snowfields everywhere, but not a complete covering, and there was low cloud and mist. We hopped about, stamped our feet and flapped our arms. In this, Greenland's warmest month, I was as cold, if not colder, than I'd ever been on any Scottish mountaintop in winter.

2   Glad of something to keep my mind off the biting wind, I told Tom about the selkies of Orkney folklore, seal-like creatures that could shed their skins and walk as men. Whether or not these selkies were really Eskimos in kayaks is impossible to say, but there are more solid accounts of what were known as fin-men. Here is the Reverend James Wallace, Minister of Kirkwall in the Orkney Islands, writing towards the end of the 17th century:

3   'Sometime about this country I see those men which are called fin-men. In 1682 one was seen sometimes sailing, sometimes rowing up and down in his little boat at the south end of the isle. Most people of the isle flocked to see him and he presently fled away most swiftly.'

4   In 1760, another minister, Francis Gatrell, records a sighting in the River Don at Aberdeen, of a canoe seven yards long and two feet wide with a man in it 'who was all over hairy and spoke a language which no person could interpret. He lived but three days though all possible care was taken to recover him.'

5   This very kayak can be seen today in the Anthropological Museum of Aberdeen University. The design of the craft places it as having come from the same waters in which we were now paddling.

6   'How could anyone paddle all the way from Greenland?' Carol wanted to know. 'Personally I need a break after two or three hours of paddling. How could someone, even driven by a storm, paddle … what … two or three weeks non-stop?'

7   We speculated about this. Perhaps they became lost in fog while out hunting, or drifted further than they realised on ice floes and, paddling eastwards, thought they were returning to the west coast of Greenland. Remembering that the 16th and 17th centuries experienced what was almost another mini Ice Age, it is possible that they found icebergs in mid ocean on which to haul out and rest. Dutch and Scandinavian whalers and traders were in the habit of kidnapping Eskimos, often lifting them out of the sea while still in their kayaks. So another possibility is that the Scottish sightings were of escaping Inuit trying to make it back to Greenland.

8   'And also we Greenland guys are pretty tough!' came Valdemar's voice from behind us.

9   Since he'd paddled quite happily the whole day without mitts and gloves, we heartily agreed.

10 'I wonder if any of them ever made it back here,' Tom mused.

11 We thought it unlikely. Not only was it against the prevailing wind and current, but also Eskimo oral tradition has proved to be both accurate and enduring and there are no tales of this kind.

Your task

Read the extract from *Fallen Pieces of the Moon* on pages 95–96 and answer the questions below.

1 Look at the first paragraph. Identify a simile and explain how it helps you to picture the rock where they landed.

2 'The main Ice Age, which had scoured this land like a giant file 8–12000 years ago, had picked the landscape clean, leaving only the Earth's ancient, bare bones.' (paragraph 2)

   Explain what you think the writer means by 'the Earth's ancient bare bones.'

3 'There are more solid accounts of what were known as fin-men.' (paragraph 2)
   ● Give three pieces of evidence from the passage which suggest that Greenlanders (also known as Eskimos or Inuit) reached Scotland in kayaks.
   ● Which of these pieces of evidence do you find most convincing as evidence of Greenlanders in Scotland? Give reasons for your choice.

4 'We speculated about this.' (paragraph 7)
   ● What does 'speculated' mean and how can you tell?
   ● What does the writer mean by 'this'? (Look at the paragraph before.)
   ● Explain how the rest of the paragraph follows from the topic sentence 'We speculated about this.'

5 'We thought it unlikely.' (paragraph 11)
   ● What does the writer mean by 'it' in this sentence?
   ● Explain how the rest of the paragraph follows from this topic sentence.

6 Why does Carol find it so surprising that Greenlanders could have reached Scotland? (paragraph 6)

7 The writer and his companions come up with two theories about how the Greenlanders could have managed to reach Scotland.
   ● What are they?
   ● Which of these theories do you find most convincing? Give reasons for your choice.

8 'Eskimo oral tradition has proved to be both accurate and enduring and there are no tales of this kind.' (paragraph 11)
   What does 'oral tradition' mean and how can you tell?

9 Give two reasons from the passage why it is unlikely that Greenlanders who reached Scotland would ever return.

7 Giving your views

You are learning:
- to form your own point of view and to give reasons for that viewpoint.

What makes someone Scottish? Can you belong to more than one country? To present your own views about a topic such as this you will need to support them with reasons.

Biography

Bashabi Fraser was born in West Bengal, India and grew up in London. She now lives in Edinburgh. In her poetry she looks at the two different worlds she experiences.

Activity 1

In this poem by Bashabi Fraser, the daughter of an Indian mother who lives in Scotland is being asked to define her national identity.

'Do' care'

In a Paris hotel lounge on one occasion
My thirteen-year-old five-foot-five
Daughter glowed with the attention
Of three young men striving
To pigeon-hole her Scottishness
And break her brittle brusqueness
With their far-eastern finesse.

If Scotland played England
Whom would she support?
Sco'land – was the answer delivered.
And if England played India?
India – she claimed with triumphant swagger.
If England played Germany?
Germany – was the response
From the unassailable position
Of a new-found nationalism.

And what if it were Scotland and India?
One demanded with the diabolical confidence
Of an argument-winning lawyer –
She clamped down her glass, shrugged her bare
Shoulders, turned away saying – do' care.

2 Why does the poet's daughter reply 'Sco'land' and not 'Scotland' to the first question?

3 Look at the answers the poet's daughter gives to the three questions she is asked in the second verse. What answers would *you* give to these questions? Are any of them different from the answers she gives and if so, why?

4 The girl in the poem answers 'Do' care' to the final question. Is she saying she does or doesn't care about the result of a Scotland versus India game? Explain your answer.

Activity 2

The girl in the poem believes that she can be both Scottish and Indian. The young men think she should choose one or the other.

Write a paragraph saying whether you agree with the girl's point of view or the men's. Remember to give reasons for your answer. Use as many of the linking words ('connectives') from the word list below as you can.

Activity 3

Research: when have Scotland ever played India at a sport? Which sport were they playing?

Knowledge about language: Connectives

Connectives join words, phrases or simple sentences together. They can add information, show contrast or show cause and effect. Use a table like the one below to sort the connectives in the word list.

Connectives for comparing	Connectives for contrasting
equally	whereas

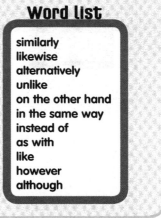

Word list

similarly
likewise
alternatively
unlike
on the other hand
in the same way
instead of
as with
like
however
although

8 Considering others' views

You are learning:
- to think about different viewpoints and say to what extent you agree with them.

If you don't sound Scottish are you still Scottish? How important are accent and language for Scottish identity? When thinking about a topic it is important to consider other people's points of view and decide whether or not you agree with them.

Activity 1

1 Read the poem below by Jackie Kay.

Old Tongue

When I was eight, I was forced south.
Not long after, when I opened
my mouth, a strange thing happened.
I lost my Scottish accent.
Words fell off my tongue:
eedyit, dreich, wabbit, crabbit
stummer, teuchter, heidbanger,
so you are, so am ur, see you, see ma ma,
shut yer geggie or I'll gie you the malkie!

My own vowels started to stretch like my bones
and I turned my back on Scotland.
Words disappeared in the dead of night,
new words marched in: *ghastly, awful,*
quite dreadful, scones said like *stones.*
Pokey hats into *ice cream cones.*
Oh where did all my words go –
my old words, my lost words?

Did you ever feel sad when you lost a word,
did you ever try and call it back
like calling in the sea?
If I could have found my words wandering,
I swear I would have taken them in,
swallowed them whole, knocked them back.
Out in the English soil, my old words
buried themselves. It made my mother's blood boil.

I cried one day with the wrong sound in my mouth.
I wanted them back; I wanted my old accent back,
my old tongue. My *dour soor* Scottish tongue.
Sing-songy. I wanted to *gie it laldie.*

Biography

Jackie Kay 1961 –
Jackie Kay was born in Edinburgh to a Scottish mother and a Nigerian father. She was adopted by a white couple at birth and was brought up in Glasgow. Her poems have appeared in many anthologies, and she has written widely for stage and television.

2 Did the writer stop being Scottish because she lived in England and started to speak with an English accent? Give your opinion with reasons.

Activity 2

For each of the following scenarios, explain what you think the child's nationality should be – or whether she has more than one.

1. A child (born in the USA) with a Scottish mother and an American father.

2. A child with Scottish parents who was born in Germany, speaks German and has never been to Scotland.

3. A child born in Scotland who moves to England with her Scottish parents.

4. A child with an English father and a Scottish mother; born in America and has never been to Britain.

Activity 3

Compare your view about the nationality of Child 2 and Child 4 with international law as explained below. Do you agree with the laws? Write a paragraph explaining why or why not.

USA: If one of your parents is American or you were born in America you are entitled to be a US national. You can have another nationality as well so Child 4 could have a British passport as well as an American one.

Germany: A person with German parents is German. Child 2 would not be German. If she wanted to be German she would have to give up her British passport.

Self-evaluation

Can you explain an argument and say whether or not you agree with it?

Choose the traffic light which best describes your level of confidence.

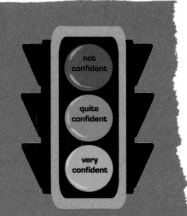

not confident

quite confident

very confident

9 Describing places

You are learning:
- to comment on a writer's choice of words.

A good description builds up a clear picture in the reader's mind. The writer's choice of words is crucial to the description.

Activity 1

The following extract is by George Mackay Brown, describing October in Orkney, where he lived.

Look for 'the Peedie Summer'

1 After gentle pacific yesterday, what a wild storm is raging outside as I write this! In the garden beyond Farafield Lane, the trees are surging, and but for their roots would be up and off, helter-skelter! Waves are breaking gray and white against the piers. The windows are awash with continuous rain.

2 Is there a lingering tent on the Ness campsite? I hope not, on a wild raging slut of a day like this.

3 The children, on holiday, will all be indoors with their computer games and word processors.

4 A good day to be sitting at the end of a long bar, drinking Guinness, working up a slow hunger for haddock and chips.

5 Many a Stromnessian, going for errands before the shops shut on Thursday afternoon, will be saying, 'Here's winter!'

6 But in fact winter is a long way off, still. Between now and the snowmen (and the 'merry dancers' and lamp-lighting at 3 o'clock) there always comes a halcyon interlude, known in Orkney as 'the peedie summer'. We can expect it at the end of October or the beginning of November – a sequence of mild sun-filled days, when we can walk about without coats or scarves; there may even be a few gentle complaints about the unseasonable mildness.

Biography

George Mackay Brown 1921–1996

George Mackay Brown is considered one of the great Scottish poets of the 20th century. He was born on Stromness in the Orkney Islands and spent most of his life in his native islands, the main source of his inspiration.

7 Make the most of that lovely interlude when it comes.

8 For one day we will wake to a wilder yelling of winds, and the driving rain will have in every little drop a little stinging core of ice, and there will be a moan and a snarl in the wrecking harbour waves.

9 Then it will be time to dig in the clothes cupboard for winter woollies, and fish the hot water bottle from under the summer debris (wondering, 'Has the rubber perished? Will it last till February?').

10 One of the chief joys of this stormy autumn day will be to set the fire to a merry blaze in late afternoon.

1 Look at the first paragraph again. List the words and expressions which suggest how violent the weather is.

2 What does 'pacific' mean (paragraph 1) and how can you tell this from the passage?

3 'A halcyon interlude.' (paragraph 6) Does halcyon mean:
   a stormy
   b calm?
   How can you tell?

4 What does Brown mean by 'merry dancers' (paragraph 6)? Use page 88 to help you find out.

Knowledge about language: Simile, metaphor and personification

A simile compares one thing with another using the words *like* or *as*. Instead of using *like* or *as*, a metaphor actually states that one thing *is* another thing. Personification is metaphor or simile where an object is spoken of as though it were alive. For example, 'The sun is smiling on the hills.'

Look again at the extract by George Mackay Brown.

1 Give one example of personification from paragraph 1.

2 Give two examples of personification from paragraph 8.

3 Using personification, describe the sun and the breeze on a mild pleasant day.

They fight like cat and dog.

Your room's a tip!

The sun is smiling on the hills

10 Imagery

You are learning:
● to appreciate a writer's use of imagery.

Writers use a range of techniques to express their ideas and create images in the minds of readers. Such techniques include metaphors, similes and personification.

Activity 1

1   The following poem, 'Blessing' was written by Imtiaz Dharker, who grew up in Glasgow. It describes a scene in India.

Biography

Imtiaz Dharker 1954–
Imtiaz Dharker is a poet and documentary film-maker. She was born in Lahore to Pakistani parents and brought up in Glasgow.

Blessing

The skin cracks like a pod.
There never is enough water.

Imagine the drip of it,
the small splash, echo
in a tin mug,
the voice of a kindly god.

Sometimes, the sudden rush
of fortune. The municipal pipe bursts,
silver crashes to the ground
and the flow has found
a roar of tongues. From the huts,
a congregation: every man, woman,
child for streets around
butts in, with pots,
brass, copper, aluminium,
plastic buckets,
frantic hands,
and naked children
screaming in the liquid sun,
their highlights polished to perfection,
flashing light,
as the blessing sings
over their small bones.

2 Copy and complete the table below to show how Dharker uses imagery in her poem 'Blessing'.

Quotation	Refers to	What this suggests
'voice of a kindly god'	the sound of water dripping	
'rush of fortune'		'fortune' suggests both that it is worth a lot to them and they are lucky this has happened
	water pouring from the burst pipe onto the ground	suggests both the colour of the water and how valuable it is
'congregation'		suggests that fetching water is a religious act
'blessing'		

Activity 2

Think about a place you know well. It could be where you live or a place you have visited often. Imagine it at a particular time of year – sunny or stormy. Write a paragraph describing it, using metaphors and similes to enhance your description.

Peer evaluation

1 Mark your paragraph from Activity 2 using the criteria below.

Beginner	Competent	Expert
The writer clearly conveys a setting and uses metaphors and/or similes.	The writer conveys an accurate and convincing impression of the setting. Good metaphors and similes are used.	The writer conveys an accurate and convincing impression of the setting. Original and very effective metaphors and similes are used.

2 Now do the same with a partner's work.

11 Fact and opinion

You are learning:
- how writers use facts and opinions to create lively and interesting accounts of places.

Good travel writing gives facts but also includes the writer's opinions about a place. Look again at page 14 to remind yourself of the difference between facts and opinions.

Activity 1

1   Read the following description of Inverness by the American writer Bill Bryson.

We rode through a pleasant but unexciting landscape. All my previous experience of the Highlands was up the more dramatic west coast, and this was decidedly muted in comparison – rounded hills, flat farms, occasional glimpses of an empty, steel-grey sea – but by no means disagreeable. I bought a cup of coffee and and a packet of biscuits from the trolley and waited for Inverness to appear.

I like Inverness immediately. It is never going to win any beauty contests, but it has some likeable features – an old-fashioned cinema called La Scala, a well-preserved market arcade, a large and adorably over-the-top nineteenth-century sandstone castle on a hill, some splendid river walks. I was particularly taken with the dim-lit market arcade. It had a barbershop with a revolving pole out front and pictures inside of people who looked like they had modelled their hairstyles on *Thunderbirds* characters. There was even a joke shop selling useful and interesting items that I hadn't seen for years: sneezing powder and plastic vomit (very handy for saving seats on trains) and chewing gum that turns the teeth black. It was shut but I made a mental note to return in the morning to stock up.

Above all, Inverness has an especially fine river, green and sedate and charmingly overhung with trees, lined on one side by big houses, trim little parks, and the old sandstone castle (now the home of the regional sheriff's courts) and on the other by big old hotels with steep-pitched roofs, more big houses and the stolid Notre Dame-like grandeur of the cathedral, standing in a broad lawn beside the river.

I regret to say I could never live in Inverness because of two sensationally ugly modern office buildings that stand by the central bridge and blot the town centre beyond any hope of redemption.

I came upon them now as I returned to the town centre and was positively riveted with astonishment to realize that an entire town could be ruined by two inanimate structures. Everything about them – scale, materials, design – was madly inappropriate to the surrounding scene. They weren't just ugly and large but so ill-designed that you could actually walk round them at least twice without ever finding the front entrance. In the larger of the two, on the river side where there might have been a restaurant or at least shops and offices with a view, much of the road frontage had been given over to a huge delivery bay with overhead metal doors. This in a building that overlooked one of the handsomest rivers in Britain. It was awful, awful beyond words.

2 Write down three facts about Inverness from this extract.

3 Write down three opinions about Inverness from this extract.

4 List five things the writer likes about Inverness.

5 Explain in your own words what the writer dislikes about Inverness.

Activity 2

The writer uses hyperbole to make his description more entertaining. For example he says, 'they blot the town centre beyond any hope of redemption.' This suggests that the town centre is doomed in an almost religious sense. In reality, town centres can function perfectly well even if there are ugly buildings there.

Find four expressions in the last paragraph which show the writer's opinion in an exaggerated and humorous way.

Explanations

Hyperbole **exaggerated and extreme language**

Knowledge about language: Adjectives

In the passage above, Bill Bryson uses adjectives to make his writing more vivid.

List five adjectives from the passage that you found particularly useful in helping you picture Inverness.

Writing Activity
functional writing

Where I live

In this unit you have read a range of texts around the theme of Scotland's cultures. You have read texts where authors write about places (Scotland, India, Greenland) reflecting on what these places are like, and making them vivid to their readers.

Your task

Imagine that your school has a weblink with another school in another part of the world. You have been asked to write a web page describing your local area to them.

In your web page you should:

- describe your area as vividly as possible, using adjectives metaphors and similes to allow readers who have never been there to imagine it

- describe the weather so that readers who are used to a different climate can imagine what it is like to be there

- describe the language of your area – explain words and expressions which are used locally and which English-speaking people from another country might not know

- say what you like about your local area and whether there are any drawbacks about living there. You might like to use humour and hyperbole to make your writing more entertaining.

Think about how you are going to make your article interesting for your readers.

Remember to use a range of sentences with a variety of connectives to develop your ideas and make your writing interesting.

5 Scottish poetry

Experiences and outcomes

In this unit you will:

Reading
- use active reading strategies to make sense of texts
- recognise how writers' language choices can enhance meaning
- look at how the form of a poem adds to its meaning
- distinguish between the attitudes of writers and their characters.

Writing
- collect, choose and bring together ideas in a plan
- write about a text, taking account of the needs of your audience
- use evidence from a poem to explain your ideas
- understand how to use comparatives and superlatives.

Spelling
- make plurals with *-es*, *-y* and *-f* endings
- look at the spelling of common homophones.

Talking and Listening
- identify and report the main points of a discussion
- work together to solve problems and share ideas
- take on a range of roles in discussions.

By the end of this unit you will:
- select poems for a specific audience with assigned group roles (Talking and Listening: Group discussion)
- analyse a poem (Reading: Textual analysis)
- write a structured essay about poetry (Writing: Critical essay).

1 Narrative poems

You are learning:
- to understand how a poem can tell a story.

A ballad is a song or poem that has been passed on by word of mouth, rather than in printed form. *Sir Patrick Spens* is an old Scottish ballad made up of details from several stories. It is loosely based on the events at the end of the 1200s when Margaret, the Maid of Norway, was heiress to the Scottish throne after the death of Alexander III. The story tells of the dramatic and tragic sea journey to bring the new queen home.

While the spelling of words in *Sir Patrick Spens* has changed over the years, most of the words are understandable if read out in a Scottish accent.

Activity 1

1 Read the poem out loud as a class.

Sir Patrick Spens

1 The king sits in Dumfermline toun
Drinking the bluid-red wine:
'O whaur will I get a skeely skipper
To sail this ship of mine?'

2 Then up and spak an eldern knicht,
Sat at the king's richt knee,
'Sir Patrick Spens is the best sailor
That sails upon the sea.'

3 The king has written a braid letter,
And seal'd it wi' his hand,
And sent it to Sir Patrick Spens,
Was walkin' on the strand.

4 The first line that Sir Patrick read,
A loud lauch lauchèd he;
The neist line that Sir Patrick read,
The teir blinded his e'e.

5 'O wha is this has dune this deid,
This ill deid dune to me,
To send me oot this time o' the yeir,
To sail upon the sea!

6 'Mak hast, mak haste, my mirry men all,
Our guid ship sails the morne,'
'O say na sae, my master deir,
For I feir a deidlie storme.

7 'Late late yestre'en I saw the new moone,
Wi' the auld moone in her arme,
And I feir, I feir, my master deir,
That we will cum to harme.'

8 O our Scots nobles wer richt laith
To weet their cork-heild schoone;
Bot lang owre a' the play wer playd,
Their hats they swam aboone.

9 O lang, lang may their ladies sit,
Wi their fans into their hand,
Or e'er they se Sir Patrick Spens
Cum sailing to the land.

10 Half owre, half owre to Aberdour,
It's fiftie fadom deip,
And thair lies guid Sir Patrick Spens,
Wi the Scots lords at his feit.

2 Make a list in bullet points of all the things that happen in the poem. If it helps, think of the poem as a series of pictures.

3 Which of the verses are the most dramatic and exciting? What makes you think so?

Activity 2

1 Make a list of all the people mentioned in the poem.

2 Who are the bravest characters in the poem? Does the poem make us try to like some of them more than others? Explain your answers.

3 What is the impression of Sir Patrick Spens himself? What is it about him that makes him seem a hero?

Activity 3

1 In ballads, sometimes the story is told by direct speech – by people in the poem. Find places in the poem where the story seems to be told by direct speech. Pick out some words spoken by the king, a knight, Sir Patrick Spens and one of his sailors.

2 Can you find any lines or phrases that are repeated? One reason for repeating lines or phrases was to help the performer remember the lines. Try to memorise a verse and see if the repetition helps.

3 This version of the ballad is written in Scots. Find examples of:
   a Scots words that are close to words we use (for example, 'bluid').
   b Scots words that are very different from the words that we would use (for example, 'schoone'). Look them up in a Scots dictionary and find what they mean.
   c Find some Scots words in the poem that you think are very lively and descriptive.

2 Rhyme

You are learning:
- to appreciate the ways in which poets use rhyme.

When poetry rhymes, we say that it has a rhyme scheme. This is the pattern made by the rhyme. To help us work out the pattern of the rhyme it is useful to give the rhyming sounds a name or letter, such as a, b, c, d and so on. When two lines rhyme next to each other, we call them a rhyming couplet.

Activity 1

1 Read the verses from 'Young Lochinvar' out loud. They are part of a ballad written by Sir Walter Scott and tells of a dramatic and romantic rescue. When you are reading, notice how the rhyme helps to create the pace and energy of the poem.

2 Make a list of all the things that happen in the poem so that you have a clear grasp of the story.

3 Write down some words to describe the action and mood of the poem. At what pace would you suggest that someone reads the poem?

Young Lochinvar

		rhyme scheme
1	Oh, young Lochinvar is come out of the west,	a
	Through all the wide Border his steed was the best;	a
	And, save his good broadsword, he weapons had none;	b
	He rode all unarm'd, and he rode all alone.	b
	So faithful in love, and so dauntless in war,	c
	There never was knight like the young Lochinvar!	c
2	He stay'd not for brake, and he stopp'd not for stone,	
	He swam the Esk river wherè ford there was none;	
	But, ere he alighted at Netherby gate,	
	The bride had consented, the gallant came late:	
	For a laggard in love, and a dastard in war,	
	Was to wed the fair Ellen of brave Lochinvar!	
3	So boldly he entered the Netherby Hall,	
	Among bridesmen, and kinsmen, and brothers, and all.	
	Then spoke the bride's father, his hand on his sword,	
	(For the poor craven bridegroom said never a word)	
	'Oh come ye in peace here, or come ye in war?	
	Or to dance at our bridal, young Lord Lochinvar?'	

4 'I long woo'd your daughter, my suit you denied –
   Love swells like the Solway, but ebbs like its tide –
   And now am I come, with this lost love of mine,
   To lead but one measure, drink one cup of wine.
   There be maidens in Scotland, more lovely by far,
   That would gladly be bride to the young Lochinvar!'

5 The bride kiss'd the goblet, the knight took it up,
   He quaff'd off the wine, and he threw down the cup.
   She look'd down to blush, and she look'd up to sigh,
   With a smile on her lips, and a tear in her eye.
   He took her soft hand, ere her mother could bar –
   'Now tread we a measure!' said young Lochinvar.

Activity 2

1 The rhyme scheme is shown for verse 1. Work out the rhyme scheme for the rest of the verses. Can you see any patterns?

2 Some of the rhymes in this poem rhyme exactly: for example *west/best*. Some are not complete rhymes. *none/alone* is an example of what is called half-rhyme.

   a Find some other examples of rhyme and half-rhyme in the poem.
   b Why do you think poets might use half-rhyme?
   c Choose any two rhyming couplets from the poem. In each couplet change one of the rhyming words, but keep the same meaning. You could use a thesaurus to help change the rhyming words. What difference does it make to the effect of the lines?

Self-evaluation

You are learning how rhyme contributes to a poem's meaning. Look at your work in the activities above and use the table to describe your abilities. Try to work out one thing that you can do to improve.

Beginner	Competent	Expert
I can see the shape of a poem. I can describe what the poem is about.	I can find the rhymes in the poem. I can see how rhyme helps the poem move at pace.	I can explain in detail how rhyme helps the rhythm of the poem.

3 Rhyme and repetition

You are learning:

● how rhyme and repetition contribute to a poem's effect.

Poets often repeat words or phrases in a poem to emphasise an important idea or to reinforce a message. The use of repetition often gives a poem shape and creates rhythm. This makes the poem more memorable and helps it to flow when you read it aloud.

Activity 1

1   Read the poem 'From a Railway Carriage' by Robert Louis Stevenson, which describes what he sees on a journey on a steam train.

From A Railway Carriage

Faster than fairies, faster than witches,
Bridges and houses, hedges and ditches;
And charging along like troops in a battle,
All through the meadows the horses and cattle:
All of the sights of the hill and the plain
Fly as thick as driving rain;
And ever again, in the wink of an eye,
Painted stations whistle by.
Here is a child who clambers and scrambles,
All by himself and gathering brambles;
Here is a tramp who stands and gazes;
And here is the green for stringing the daisies!
Here is a cart run away in the road
Lumping along with man and load;
And here is a mill, and there is a river:
Each a glimpse and gone forever!

2 Make a list of the things the poet sees from the window.

3 Which words and phrases in the poem create a sense of speed? Make a list.

5 The last line of the poem is an interesting conclusion. Explain the idea behind this line.

Activity 2

1 A syllable is a unit of sound that can be a whole word or part of a word. Write out a line of the poem and show the syllables like this:

> Fast-er than fair-ies, fast-er than wit-ches

2 Underline the syllables which have a stronger beat (a stronger beat means those syllables have more emphasis than others when they are spoken). See if this pattern is repeated in the poem.

3 This poem makes effective use of rhythm. Can you see what the pattern of the poem is trying to imitate?

4 Write a couple of lines of your own in the same rhythm, describing what you might see from a train window. Try to make it rhyme as well.

Activity 3

Look at the previous two poems in this unit. Copy some lines from them and show how they use a regular rhythm too.

Knowledge about language: Comparative and superlative adjectives

Poems can tell dramatic stories or be about strong and intense feelings. Adjectives can be used to describe and compare things. Superlatives are used to show the most extreme comparison. Comparatives and superlatives are made by adding -er or -est.

1 Here are some comparatives and superlatives:

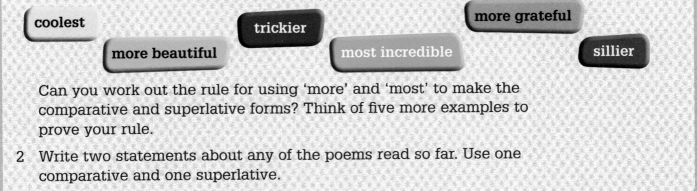

coolest   more beautiful   trickier   most incredible   more grateful   sillier

Can you work out the rule for using 'more' and 'most' to make the comparative and superlative forms? Think of five more examples to prove your rule.

2 Write two statements about any of the poems read so far. Use one comparative and one superlative.

4 Active reading

You are learning:
- to use active reading strategies to make sense of texts.

An exciting feature of poetry is that there are so many meanings to be found within each poem. As long as we can explain our ideas about a poem and support them with evidence, then our ideas are valid.

Activity 1

1 Read the poem out loud. ('Broukit' means 'neglected'.)

The Bonnie Broukit Bairn

Mars is braw in crammasy,
Venus in a green silk goun,
The auld mune shaks her gowden feathers,
Their starry talk's a wheen o' blethers,
Nane for thee a thochtie sparin',
Earth, thou bonnie broukit bairn!
– *But greet, an in your tears ye'll droun*
The haill clanjamfrie!

Biography

Hugh MacDiarmid 1892–1978
Hugh MacDiarmid is one of the most significant poets of the 20th century. He was born in Langholm in the Borders and, although he mostly wrote in English, writing in Scots was very important to him as well. For most of his life he was a journalist and it was only later in life that he made enough money from writing to do it full time. The long Scots poem 'A Drunk Man Looks at the Thistle' is probably his best known work. Some of his shorter poems might seem simple but under closer examination they have a deeper meaning.

2 The word 'crammasy' is Scots for an expensive deep red cloth. The reference to the 'mune' shaking her 'gowden feathers' (line 4) often makes people think that the moon is like a bird. It could also be a reference to women wearing ostrich feathers as a fashion accessory – something that was more common in the 1930s when this poem was written.

Hugh MacDiarmid describes three planets and the moon in this poem. Make a list of the three planets and describe in your own words what they are wearing. You could draw them if you prefer.

Activity 2

A personification is a figure of speech. It means that an object that is not alive or human has been written about as if it is. The planets and the moon in this poem are personifications.

1 Look at the kinds of clothes that each planet wears and the description that you have written. What do you think is being suggested about each planet?

2 What is different about the description of the Earth?

3 What is it that makes the Earth different from the other planets and the moon?

4 Explain what you think the line 'Nane for thee a thochtie sparin'' might mean. What does it suggest about the poet's attitude towards the Earth?

Activity 3

1 The last two lines of the poem are set apart from the rest of the poem.
  a What is the effect of the word 'but' when you see it at the start of the line?
  b What can the Earth do that the other planets cannot? Why do you think that this is important?

2 Hugh MacDiarmid deliberately chose to write in Scots and was trying to use Scots at a time when many people were not writing in it. Make a list of the Scots words in this poem.

3 Write a short paragraph defending MacDiarmid's choice to use Scots. Try to explain why words like *greet, broukit, wheen, blethers, clanjamfrie* work better than phrases that Standard English might provide.

5 Imagery

One of the best ways to make an image clear is by comparing it to something that the reader can understand. A **simile** compares two things using the word *like* or *as*: He's as cool as a cucumber.

A **metaphor** is when we simply say an object is something else: Your room's a tip!

He's as cool as a cucumber.

Your room's a tip!

Activity 1

'Red Running Shoes' by Jackie Kay is a poem that uses visual images to make the reader see a scene clearly in their mind.

1   Read the poem. Look out for similes as you are reading.

Red Running Shoes

I wore some other girl's red running shoes
with real spikes like rose thorns under my foot.

I got into position: my limbs seriously tense,
one knee on the asphalt, one foot flat, all that.

I crouched over, hands down, like a predator
ready for prey; and took off, took flight

on the red running track, so fast I could be fear
running, a live fright, a chance vision.

My dark hair wild in the wind.
My arms pounding light years, thin air, euphoria.

I flew past in some other girl's red running shoes
round the red track, near the railway line.

I raced straight towards the future.
The past was left standing behind, waving.

I ran and ran; my feet became the land.
I couldn't tell if the ground was moving under my feet

shifting sand, or if I might just stop like a heartbeat.
It felt as if I could run for ever, hard pounding feet

Until I ran right into myself, years on, sat still, heavy,
past forty, groaning, the streak lightning
gone.

2 At first the poem seems to be about a young girl running in a race. Pick out all of the words and phrases that show that she is really trying to do well and run fast.

3 How does the girl feel when she is running? Select the quotations that support your ideas.

4 In the last four verses of the poem, there are several references to time.
 a Pick them out.
 b What seems to be strange about these references to time in a poem about a race?

5 At the end of the poem how does the girl feel?

Activity 2

Find the similes in the poem. Explain why you think they are effective. Think about what is being compared and what image it brings to mind.

Activity 3

1 In this poem, the girl's life is being compared to a race. What does that suggest about how she feels about her life?

2 Can you think of any other images that we could compare our lives to? You could make them into similes starting 'My life is like …'

Self-evaluation

You are learning to know and use the terms for analysing poetry. Decide how well you think you can do this and think about how you might improve.

Beginner	Competent	Expert
I can identify some imagery.	I can identify imagery and comment on what it means.	I can identify imagery and make comments about its effectiveness.

6 Writers' language choices

You are learning:

- to analyse a writer's language choices and explore their effect.

Robert Burns wrote in the Scots language at a time when it was not fashionable to do so.

Biography

Robert Burns 1759–1796
Robert Burns was born in Alloway, Ayrshire. He was a farmer before he became famous as a poet. He produced hundreds of poems and songs that are still popular today. His birthday (25th January) is celebrated in 'Burns Suppers' where his works are performed, his life discussed and traditional Scottish foods are eaten. For many people, Burns represents Scotland and what it means to be Scottish.

Activity 1

It was while Burns was ploughing one of his fields that he disturbed a mouse's nest. His thoughts on what he had done led to one of his best-known poems, 'To a Mouse'.

1   Read the poem.

To a Mouse

On turning her up in her nest with the plough, November 1785.

1 Wee, sleekit, cowrin, tim'rous beastie,
O, what a panic's in thy breastie!
Thou need na start awa sae hasty
            Wi' bickering brattle!
I wad be laith to rin an' chase thee,
            Wi' murdering pattle.

2 I'm truly sorry Man's dominion
Has broken Nature's social union,
An' justifies that ill opinion
            Which makes thee startle
At me, thy poor, earth-born companion
            An' fellow mortal!

3 I doubt na, whyles, but thou may thieve;
What then? poor beastie, thou maun live!
A daimen icker in a thrave
            'S a sma' request;
I'll get a blessin wi' the lave,
            An' never miss't!

4 Thy wee-bit housie, too, in ruin!
It's silly wa's the win's are strewin!
An' naething, now, to big a new ane,
            O' foggage green!
An' bleak December's win's ensuin,
            Baith snell an' keen!

5 Thou saw the fields laid bare an' waste,
   An' weary winter comin fast,
   An' cozie here, beneath the blast,
         Thou thought to dwell,
   Till crash! the cruel coulter past
         Out thro' thy cell.

6 That wee bit heap o' leaves an' stibble,
   Has cost thee monie a weary nibble!
   Now thou's turned out, for a' thy trouble,
         But house or hald,
   To thole the winter's sleety dribble,
         An' cranreuch cauld.

7 But Mousie, thou art no thy-lane,
   In proving foresight may be vain:
   The best laid schemes o' mice an' men
         Gang aft agley,
   An' lea'e us nought but grief an' pain,
         For promis'd joy!

8 Still thou are blest, compared wi' me!
   The present only toucheth thee:
   But och! I backward cast my e'e,
         On prospects drear!
   An' forward, tho' I canna see,
         I guess an' fear!

2 Robert Burns is speaking to the mouse in this poem. He tries to show us how small and vulnerable the mouse is by the way that he describes the mouse and its home. Pick out some of the words and phrases that Burns uses to describe the mouse and its nest. Explain how they suggest that the mouse is small and weak.

3 Find the verse where the plough destroys the mouse's nest. How does Burns use alliteration in this verse?

Explanations

> **Alliteration when words start with the same consonant sound.**

Activity 2

In this poem, Robert Burns is also showing us how harsh it was to live and work on a farm in the Scottish winter.

1 Pick out some of the words and phrases which he uses to describe the weather or the wintry setting of this poem.

2 Explain how these Scots words help us feel and see the cold of winter.

Activity 3

Read the last two verses again. Here Burns stops describing the mouse's life and discusses his own. He says that human lives are as sad and precarious as the mouse's, more so in some ways.

1 What words in verse 7 describe the feelings that we have when good plans go wrong?

2 What words does Burns use when he describes his own future in verse 8?

3 How would you read out the last two verses? Think about which words and phrases should be emphasised, and where there should be pauses. Explain where it should be loud – and quiet – and describe the kind of voice in which it should be read.

7 Looking at audience

You are learning:
- to understand how audiences and readers choose and respond to texts.

When different people read the same poems and other texts they often see different things. It is interesting to hear how other people interpret poems so we can deepen our own understanding. It is important to explain our ideas using words or phrases from the poem to help other people understand where our thoughts come from.

Activity 1

1 Read the following extracts from some first year pupils. Look at how they write about some of the poems in this book.

A "Sir Patrick Spens" is an exciting poem with lots of action. – Andrew

B My favourite poem is "Young Lochinvar". If I wanted to make a presentation of it, I would set it to fast music to emphasise the beat." – Emma

C In "To a Mouse" Robert Burns wants us to think about how we treat nature. – David

D "The Bonnie Broukit Bairn" is important to Hugh MacDiarmid because he thinks that there are more important things than money. – Catriona

E I liked "From a Railway Carriage" because it described scenes well. – James

F I think that "To a Mouse" is about Robert Burns' own life. – Jennifer

2 Do you agree or disagree with these statements? Explain your reasons and use evidence from the poem to support your answers.

3 Which poem have you enjoyed the most? Write a paragraph about the poems you have read so far in this unit. Try to include a line from one of the poems in your response. You could use some of the following sentence starters in your paragraph:

When the poet says "_____" it makes me think about _____

I like the sound of the rhyme in this poem because _____

The poem made me wonder why _____

The line "_____" makes me feel that the poet thinks _____

The ending of the poem suggests to me that _____

4 Find out which poems other people in your class enjoyed the most and why they liked them. Is there a class favourite?

Activity 2

Working in a group, choose your favourite poem from the ones you have studied and give a talk on it. You can use this structure:

1 Introduce the poem. What was it about?

2 The reason we picked this poem is …

3 The best line or phrase in the poem is … because …

4 We think that the poet was trying to make us feel that …

5 The poet made us think (or feel) that …

When you rehearse and give your presentation, think about how you will get your message across to the audience. Think about pace, volume, gestures, expression and eye contact.

Peer evaluation

As you watch and listen to other groups' presentations, use the table below to decide which level they are working at. For each group, note one thing you think they did well and one thing which they could improve.

Beginner	Competent	Expert
The group gave a presentation.	They took an active part in a group presentation.	They used different techniques to engage an audience.
They told us some simple ideas.	They made the presentation interesting for an audience.	They used appropriate features such as pace, gesture and expression.

Talking and Listening Activity
Group discussion

Poetry performance

Your class has been asked to put on a poetry performance for Primary 7 pupils. In groups, you have to choose three or four poems that go together well, perhaps with a common theme, and decide how you are going to perform them.

Your task

Prepare a poetry performance for Primary 7 pupils. You should:

- choose a theme or a linking idea for your performance
- select three or four poems to perform
- decide how you are going to introduce your show and how you are going to perform your poems.

What to do:

- choose a theme that Primary 7 pupils will enjoy and find interesting
- choose poems that are suitable for performing
- use poems from this book, or from other books in the classroom or library, or from books you have at home, or from the internet
- the poems could be by one poet or different poets
- make your introduction interesting and exciting
- annotate the poems with notes about how it should be performed.

You will be assessed on how well you work together as a group.

- listening to each other
- coming to an agreement
- making suggestions
- building on each other's ideas
- getting the task done.

8 Writer's point of view

You are learning:
● to identify and comment on a writer's purpose and viewpoint.

There are many Scottish poets who have written about their own country. Sometimes the poems are just descriptions of the places they have seen and sometimes the poets try to describe the country as a whole and what it is like to be a Scot.

Activity 1

1 Read the extracts from a selection of poems.

What do you mean when you speak of
Scotland?
The grey defeats that are dead and gone
Behind the legends, that each generation
Savours afresh, yet can't live on.
... Scotland's an attitude of mind.
Maurice Lindsay

Scotland's image? You must be joking!
The less said about that the better.
Bagpipes and haggis.
Tyrell McConnall

Breathes there the man with soul so dead,
Who never to himself hath said,
This is my own, my native land!
Whose heart hath ne'er within him burn'd
As home his footsteps he hath turn'd
From wandering on a foreign strand!
Sir Walter Scott

England thy beauties are tame and domestic
To one who has roved on the mountains afar;
Oh for the crags that are wild and majestic!
The steep frowning glories of dark Loch na Garr.
George Gordon Byron

'Nothing but heather!'– How
marvellously descriptive!
And incomplete!
Hugh MacDiarmid

O Scotia! My dear, my native soil!
For whom my warmest wish to heaven is sent!
Long may thy hardy sons of rustic toil
Be blest with health, and peace, and sweet content.
Robert Burns

125

2 Complete a table like the one below to show which statements relate to which poet. Quote some words from the relevant poem to support each statement.

Statement	Poet	Some words in the poem supporting this
We should all be proud of our country.		
The writer is proud of Scotland's scenery.		
Scotland is a country which has a troubled past.		
The same old ideas are used to describe Scotland.		
There is a lot more to Scotland than you might think.		
The poet is proud of Scotland and Scottish people.		

3 Are any of the poets critical of Scotland? Give evidence for your answer.

Activity 2

1 Make a list of the kinds of images that are usually used to describe or represent Scotland.

2 Which of the images you listed do you think are relevant nowadays? Which of them have been around for a long time?

3 Make a list of the images that you would use to represent modern Scotland. What images would you like the world to think of when they hear the word Scotland? What things in modern Scotland do we have to be proud of?

Self-evaluation

Look at the work you have completed on the poems in this lesson. How well are you doing? Decide what you have to do to improve.

Beginner	Competent	Expert
I know what a poem is about.	I can comment on the writer's point of view.	I can comment on the writer's point of view and give some explanation of his viewpoint, using examples from the poem to support my ideas.

There/their/they're

Their, *there* and *they're* have completely different meanings.
Their means *belonging to them*.
There means *in, at* or *to a place*.
They're is short for *they are*. The apostrophe stands for the missing letter *a*.

1   Write out the following sentences, inserting the correct spelling of *their*, *there* or *they're*.

   a   The children put _____ shoes in the cupboard.

   b   In the box under the stairs _____ were six, tiny black and white kittens.

   c   'We mustn't disturb them, _____ too small at the moment,' said Dad.

Where/were/we're

These words look very similar but have different meanings.
Where can be used as an adverb to find out the place where something is.
Were is the past tense of the verb 'to be', as in:
you are (present) / *you were* (past).
We're is short for *we are*. The apostrophe stands for the missing letter *a*.

2   Write out the following sentences and fill in the missing words.

   a   'Do you know _____ my new scarf is?' asked Mum.

   b   'We put it in the box with the kittens because they _____ cold,' admitted Jake.

   c   'When we come home from school, _____ going to name them,' he continued.

   d   Meanwhile, the kittens _____ purring contentedly in _____ warm bed.

3   Write some more sentences with blanks to test a partner's understanding of *their*, *there*, *they're*, *where*, *were* and *we're*.

9 Writing about poems

You are learning:
- to write about a poem.

When we write about poems we need to explain what we think. By choosing words or phrases from the poem we can support our ideas.

Activity 1

1 Read the poem below.

Biography

Carol Ann Duffy 1955–
Carol Ann Duffy was born in Glasgow. She decided at the age of 14 that she was going to become a poet and had her first poems published when she was 18. Her poetry has won many major prizes and she was awarded a CBE in 2001. She has written plays and is widely published.

Your Dresses

I like your rain dress,
its strange, sad colour,
its small buttons like tears.

I like your fog dress,
how it swirls around you
when you dance on the lawn.

Your snow dress I like,
its million snowflakes
sewn together with a needle of ice,

but I love your thunderstorm dress,
its huge dark petticoats,
its silver stitches flashing as you run away.

2 Now answer the following questions.
   a What are your first thoughts about this poem?
   b List the different dresses and explain why the poet likes them.
   c When the poet says 'dresses', she is not talking about clothes. What is she actually referring to?
   d Why do you think she loves the thunderstorm dress more than the others?

Activity 2

When we write about poetry, it is useful to have a structure to remember to record our ideas. Try using the 'SMILE' structure below. Remember, not all poems will use all of the features.

Structure and form – how the poem is set out on the page and how this links to

Meaning – what the poem is about.

Imagery – the use of simile, metaphor and personification.

Language – words and phrases which you think are powerful.

Explain your ideas – use words or phrases to support your ideas.

1   Read 'Your Dresses' again. Use a table like the one below to record your ideas. Some sentence starters are included to help you.

Your thoughts	'Your Dresses'
Structure and form	The poet uses a different verse for….
Meaning	
Imagery	She uses some similes and metaphors. For example …
Language (pick out key words and phrases)	
Explain your own ideas about the poem.	My favourite description in the poem is … because …

2   Using the notes from your table, develop some sentences explaining your thoughts about the poem. Remember to use words or phrases from the poem to support your ideas. Make a **statement**, use a **reference** to the text and then make a **comment** showing your opinion.

3   Find the statement, the reference and the comment in this example.

4   Write your statement, reference and comment about the poem 'The Dresses'.

> Carol Ann Duffy describes the mood of each type of weather. She uses words like 'swirls' and 'dance on the lawn' to describe the fog. This made me think that she likes the way the fog seems to move quickly and create a happy atmosphere.

Peer evaluation

Look at a partner's statement, reference and comment from Activity 2, Question 4. Work out which is the statement, which is the reference and which is the comment. Check that each does the job it should:

● Does the statement identify a key feature of the poem?

● Does the reference use a quotation from the poem to support the point?

● Does the comment explain how the evidence supports the point? Does it comment on the effect it has on the reader?

10 Planning

You are learning:
- to collect, choose and bring together ideas in a plan.

When you note down your ideas after reading a poem, they may not be organised enough to express your thoughts clearly. If you make a plan, you can use it to help you choose the main points you want to make and consider the best order in which to put them.

Activity 1

1   Below is a jumbled up version of a plan for a piece of writing about the poem 'To a Mouse' by Robert Burns. Organise the points in the best order.

A The first six verses describe the mouse's life and how Burns has destroyed its nest.

B The last verse is a description of how Burns feels about his own life.

C The poet uses lots of words and phrases to make the mouse seem small and fragile.

D The poem is about how we treat the natural world.

E Finally, I liked the way the poem made me think about how we can destroy nature.

F Burns uses Scots words to talk to the mouse as if it is a friend.

2   Compare your versions with a partner's. Did you put them in the same order? How did you make decisions about the order?

3   Take each of your points and develop it into a paragraph containing at least three sentences using statement – reference – comment.

4   When you write your conclusion in the final paragraph, make sure you refer back to a point you made in the opening paragraph, then add something to that point to finish your essay.

Activity 2

Connectives will help you link ideas both within paragraphs and between paragraphs. Look at this example:

> In 'To a Mouse', Burns explains that he is personally sorry in the first person by using 'I'. However, in verse 7, he uses the plural 'us' to show the reader that people's plans can go wrong as well.

Try adding some of the following connectives to your own paragraphs.

To contrast different things in the poems

On the other hand ...
Whereas ...
However ...

To tell the reader where they are in the essay

First ...
Finally ...
In conclusion ...

To introduce examples

For example ...
For instance ...
... such as ...

To introduce explanations

This shows that ...
This suggests that ...
This implies that ...

To compare similar things in the poems

Similarly ...
In the same way ...
Equally ...

Self-evaluation

Beginner	Competent	Expert
I can group similar ideas together.	I can link paragraphs.	I can link paragraphs using a variety of connectives.
I can organise ideas logically.	I can explain ideas in detail using textual references.	I can write openings and endings that link.

Check your writing about the poems. Decide how well you are working and what you need to do to improve.

Knowledge about language: Plurals (-y and -f endings)

Words that end in -y in the singular are made plural by dropping the -y and adding -ies. For example, *pony – ponies*, *trophy – trophies*.

Words that end in -ey in the singular are made plural by adding an -s, as in *monkey – monkeys*.

Most words that end in -f in the singular are made plural by dropping the -f and adding -ves as in: *half – halves*.

Write a test for a partner listing the singular form of six words that end in -y, -ey or -f. Your partner's task is to turn them all into plurals.

Reading Activity
Analysis of two poems

Homes

The following two poems are about homes. The first is by Jackie Kay, who tries to imagine what it would be like if every room in a house had feelings. The second is by Diana Hendry, who writes about the ways in which we can hide.

Your task

Read both poems and answer the questions that follow.

No. 115 dreams

The living room remembers Gran dancing to Count Basie.
The kitchen can still hear my aunts fighting on Christmas day.
The hall is worried about the loose banister.
The small room is troubled by the missing hamster.
The toilet particularly dislikes my grandfather.
The wallpaper covers up for the whole family.

And No. 115 dreams of lovely houses by the sea.
And No. 115 dreams of one night in the country.

The stairs are keeping schtum about the broken window.
The toilet's sick of the trapped pipes squealing so.
The walls aren't thick enough for all of the screaming.
My parents' bedroom has a bed in a choppy sea.
My own bedroom loves the bones of me.
My brother's bedroom needs a different boy.

And No. 115 dreams of yellow light, an attic room.
And No. 115 dreams of a chimney, a new red roof.

And the red roof dreams of robin redbreasts
tap dancing on the red dance floor in the
open air.

Hiding Places

The world beneath the table
When no-one knows you're there,
The second home that's all your own
Underneath the stair.

Your bedroom when you shut the door
And in the mirror see
This quite fantastic person
You know you're going to be.

The space above the wardrobe
Where your best-kept secrets nest,
The attic that's a hideout when
Your parent is a pest.

The hideaway inside your head
Contains a magic light,
Just switch it on and you can zap
All monsters of the night.

A person needs a hiding place –
Four walls alone won't do.
You need a corner, secret, quiet,
To grow you into you.

1 Pick one of the rooms from the poem 'No. 115 dreams' that has a happy memory. Explain in your own words why the memory is happy.

2 Pick one of the rooms that has a less pleasant memory. Explain why you think this.

3 Which do you think is the speaker's favourite room? Why?

4 The lines in verses 1 and 3 start the same way. Why do you think Kay does this? What effect does it have?

5 The two short verses (2 and 4) tell us of what the house dreams about. What effect do these verses have?

6 Describe the image in the last verse. Why does this create a happy tone at the end of the poem?

7 Find another image from somewhere else in the poem. Say why you think it is effective.

8 What kind of person do you think is speaking in 'Hiding Places'? What age group do you think the speaker is?

9 Find any part of the poem where the poet makes a hiding place seem exciting. Which words or phrases do this?

10 The following quotations suggest something about how the speaker in 'Hiding Places' thinks and feels. Complete a table like the one below, explaining what you think each quotation means. One has been done to suggest the kind of answer you should give.

Quotation	What this tells us about the poet and how she thinks
This quite fantastic person who you know you're going to be	She uses 'fantastic' because she believes that we all have the potential to do wonderful and exciting things with our lives.
When your parent is a pest	
The hideaway inside your head	
A person needs a hiding place	

11 What do you understand by 'all monsters of the night'?

12 Explain the ideas contained in the last verse. Why does the speaker feel that being alone is important sometimes?

13 This task is about both poems.

Compare the views of home that each poem offers. You should comment on:
- the impression you get of each home
- what the place means to the poet
- how they are similar and how they contrast
- the way that structure, rhythm and language are used to create an impression.

You could end by explaining which poem you prefer and why.

6 Take action

Experiences and outcomes

In this unit you will:

Reading
- find information from different sources for a task
- compare the way information is presented.

Writing
- make brief, clearly organised notes of key points
- plan, draft, edit, revise, proofread and present a text with readers in mind
- express a personal view
- organise ideas into a sequence of paragraphs
- organise sentences in a paragraph
- vary the formality of language to suit purpose and circumstances.

Words and sentences
- use colons and semi-colons correctly
- look at prefixes
- review the use of prepositions
- use pronouns correctly to write in the first and third person
- use simple, complex and compound sentences.

Talking and Listening
- use talk as a way of researching ideas and expanding thinking
- identify and report the main points from a speech and a discussion
- identify the main methods used by presenters to explain, persuade, amuse or argue a case.

By the end of this unit you will:
- analyse a final speech (Talking and Listening Activity: Listening)
- create a leaflet to present a group's views (Writing Activity: Discursive writing).

1 Finding information

You are learning:

● how information can be presented and how to find the information you need.

We pick up information not just through words but from pictures, presentational features and the way in which they are organised.

Activity 1

This web page is from the SortIt website. This is a Scotland-wide campaign that encourages us to recycle our rubbish and help the environment.

1 Look at the list of presentational features the website designer has used to organise the information and attract the reader. Match the features in the box opposite to the numbered arrows.

2 What responses was the designer trying to create in the reader? Write a sentence about each feature to explain your answer.

a The name of the campaign
b The logo for the campaign
c Title
d Images
e Links to other pages on the site

Activity 2

It's the summer holidays. You're bored. You have persuaded a parent to take you to a theme park. They have agreed, but only on condition that you do all the organising.

Write down where you could find the answer to each of the following questions on the internet.

*   You want to go tomorrow. What will the weather be like?
*   What's the best way to get there?
*   How much will it cost?
*   The theme park's website says the café has been *refurbished*. What does that mean?

Activity 3

How can you find one piece of information in the huge range of resources that are available to you? There are lots of ways of organising information. Look at the three texts that follow, and answer the questions to practise your information-finding skills.

Text A is taken from a leaflet to encourage recycling.

Text A

Over 50% of the rubbish in our bins can be recycled, and yet:

♻ 74% of waste goes to landfill. This generates dangerous liquids and gases. Many landfill sites are nearly full and we are running out of suitable land to build new sites.

♻ 18% of waste is recycled – this saves landfill space, energy, import costs and raw materials. It also cuts air pollution.

♻ 8% of waste is incinerated – this produces smoke, ash and dangerous chemicals such as dioxins, but usually in amounts so small that they are not dangerous.

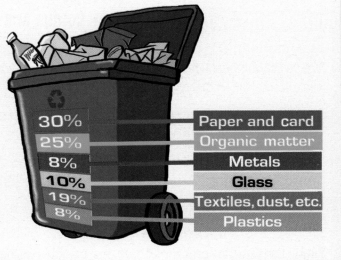

The average household bin contains:

30%	Paper and card
25%	Organic matter
8%	Metals
10%	Glass
19%	Textiles, dust, etc.
8%	Plastics

1   Diagrams can give the reader a lot of information. Use the diagram above to work out the type of waste that takes up the most space in our bins.

2 Scan Text A to answer these questions. Remember: when scanning, identify a key word in the question, then scan the text to find that word.

   a How much of our waste is put into landfill sites?

   b What is produced when waste is incinerated?

   c What does 'landfill' mean? Use Text B to help you.

Text B is part of a glossary from a website that encourages recycling.

> **Text B**
>
> **Kerbside recycling**
> Also known as **collect schemes**, these are schemes where households put recyclable material in special containers on the roadside outside their homes for collection by the local authority or a waste contractor.
>
> **Landfill**
> Most rubbish collected from homes in the UK is buried in large holes in the ground (often old quarries) called landfill sites.
>
> **Leachate**
> Liquid that drains from a landfill site. It consists of a mixture of rainwater and rotten organic materials.

3 A glossary is like a mini-dictionary: it explains the meaning of difficult words in a particular text or subject.

   a Why do some texts have a glossary?

   b What do you notice about the organisation of the key words in the glossary?

Knowledge about language: Colons and semi-colons

A colon is used to introduce something. This may be a list:
The average household bin contains: paper and card, organic matter, metal, glass, etc.

colon

1 Use a colon and a list to complete this sentence.
- Items our school could recycle include …

A semi-colon is sometimes used to join two clauses in a sentence, taking the place of a connective like *and* or *but*. So:

I love listening to loud music but the neighbours hate it.

could be written as:

I love listening to loud music ~~but~~; the neighbours hate it.

semi-colon

2 Rewrite these sentences using a semi-colon.

   a My class recycles paper and sometimes we recycle plastic.

   b We recycle in our school but not all schools recycle.

Text C is the index from a science book for pupils.

 Text C

Index

4   What do you notice about the organisation of the entries in the index?

5   How could you use Text C to help you find more information on landfill?

6   Where do you normally find the index in a book?

2 Aiming at a target audience

You are learning:
- To direct your writing and presentation to appeal to a specific audience.

We wear different clothes for different occasions – and it is important to get the right clothes for the right occasion. The same is true of the words we use: some are appropriate for a formal situation; some are more suited to an informal situation.

Activity 1

Speakers A to C are talking about recycling.

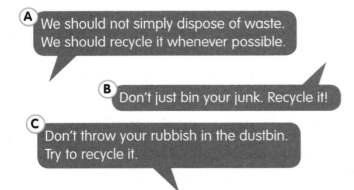

A We should not simply dispose of waste. We should recycle it whenever possible.

B Don't just bin your junk. Recycle it!

C Don't throw your rubbish in the dustbin. Try to recycle it.

1 What situation could each speaker be in?
2 Who do you think each speaker is talking to?
3 Which uses the most formal language?
4 Which uses the most informal language?

Activity 2

Many texts are written to appeal to a specific audience: the target audience. This may be people of a particular age group or with a particular interest. Look at the magazine covers on the right.

1 For each one, write a sentence describing its target audience.

2 Would you expect the language used in these magazines to be more formal or more informal?

Activity 3

On the right are extracts from two websites, explaining what climate change and global warming mean.

One of these websites says it aims to provide 'a forum for the development of pragmatic policies to address the most pressing global environmental problem of the 21st century.'

The other website says it aims to 'help you explore your environment and learn how to protect it. We've got games, pictures, and stories.'

1   Which website do you think gives which description of itself?

2   How would you describe the target audiences of these websites?

3   Compare how these extracts appeal to their target audiences. Write down what you notice about the following.

- Presentation – how the texts look. Try to comment on:
  - the use of colour
  - the use of images.
- Language – the way the writers have written the texts. Try to comment on:
  - the length of the sentences
  - the kinds of words used
  - whether the language used is formal or informal.

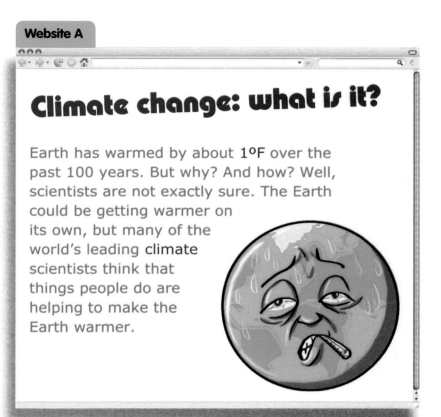

Website A

Climate change: what is it?

Earth has warmed by about 1°F over the past 100 years. But why? And how? Well, scientists are not exactly sure. The Earth could be getting warmer on its own, but many of the world's leading climate scientists think that things people do are helping to make the Earth warmer.

Website B

Global warming basics

The scientific community has reached a strong consensus regarding the science of global climate change. The world is undoubtedly warming.

This warming is largely the result of emissions of carbon dioxide and other greenhouse gases from human activities including industrial processes, fossil fuel combustion, and changes in land use, such as deforestation.

3 Identifying the main points

You are learning:
- to follow an argument by identifying the key points.

To understand and respond to an argument, you need to be able to identify the key points the writer is making.

Activity 1

Most scientists believe that we are polluting our planet and changing our climate. Some scientists disagree. They think that changes to the Earth's temperature can be explained by more natural causes. The following text supports this argument.

1 Read the text below and answer the questions on page 143 to learn how to identify the key points the writer is making.

Save the planet, eat a vegan

1 Good news. It seems that your car and your fondness for sunken light bulbs in every alcove are not warming up the planet after all.

2 In fact, according to EarthSave, methane, which pours from a cow's bottom on an industrial scale every few minutes, is 21 times more powerful as a greenhouse gas than carbon dioxide. And as a result, farmed animals are doing more damage to the climate than all the world's transport and power stations put together.

3 EarthSave is encouraging us to stop eating all forms of animal products. No more milk. No more cheese. And if it can be proven that bees fart, then no more honey either. You've got to become a vegan.

4 Now of course if you don't like the taste of meat, then it's perfectly reasonable to become a vegetablist. But becoming a vegan? Short of being paraded on the internet while wearing a fluffy pink tutu, I can think of nothing I'd like less.

5 Of course there are certain weeds I like very much. Cauliflower and leeks particularly. But these are an accompaniment to food, useful only for filling up the plate and absorbing the gravy. The idea of eating only a cauliflower, without even so much as a cheese sauce, fills me with dread.

6 So plainly the best thing we can do if we want to save the world and keep on eating meat, is to work out a way that animals can be made to produce less methane.

7 Scientists in Germany are working on a pill that helps, but apparently this has a number of side effects. These are not itemised, but I can only assume that if you trap the gas inside the cow one of the drawbacks is that it might explode. Nasty.

8 At the moment, largely, cows eat grass and silage, and as we've seen, this is melting the ice caps and killing us all. So they need a new foodstuff: something that is rich in iron, calcium and natural goodness.

9 Plainly they can't eat meat so here's an idea to chew on. Why don't we feed them vegans?

1   Look at the title of the text. Use it to write one sentence that sums up the writer's point of view.

2   Each paragraph in a text usually contains one key point. The second paragraph in the text contains 54 words. Try to sum up its key point in 15 words or less.

3   Often the key point in a paragraph is made in the first sentence. What is the key point being made in the third paragraph?

4   What is the key point in paragraph four? Did you find it in the first sentence, or did you have to read the whole paragraph to find it?

5   Re-read paragraph five. What is the key point here?

6   Paragraphs six and seven give a possible solution to the problem. What evidence is given in the text to suggest that the writer is unsure that this is an effective solution to the problem?

7   Paragraphs eight and nine give another possible solution. What does it suggest about:
    a   the writer's attitude to the problem?
    b   the writer's attitude to vegans?

Activity 2

As well as being able to identify the main points in a written text, you need to be able to identify the main points made in a discussion.

With a partner, choose one of the following topics.
• Father Christmas does not exist.
• Children should be encouraged to eat more sweets.
• The weekend should be cut to one day.

One of you will support the argument and the other will argue against it. Write down five points that will help you win the argument; do not show them to your partner.

Discuss your chosen topic with your partner, using your points to try to persuade them that your point of view is the right one. Try to:
• listen carefully to your partner
• respond to their points – don't just read out your own points
• ask them questions that will defeat their argument.

After the discussion, write down a list of the key points your partner made. Compare lists. Did you find all of each other's key points?

Knowledge about language: Prefixes

A prefix is a string of letters that can be added to the front of a word to alter its meaning. Sometimes this creates an opposite: adding *un-* to the front of *important* creates *unimportant*. *Pre-* is a prefix meaning *earlier*, *before* or *in front of*.

1   For each of the words below, write a definition that includes the word *before*.

    prepay   prearrange
    premature   preview

2   Now look at these four word endings: *-pay*, *-arrange*, *-mature*, *-view*, and suggest other prefixes that can go in front of them to create new words.

4 Getting your point across

You are learning:
- to identify persuasive language and deliver a speech effectively.

When writers or speakers argue their point of view, they do not just use their ideas to persuade us. We are also persuaded by the language they choose.

Activity 1

Below is an extract from a speech made by Charles Kennedy MP, in which he tries to persuade his audience that the Liberal Democrat party cares about environmental issues.

What price our planet?

We know people are concerned about the kind of world our children will inherit, and they are worried about the legacy we are creating for them.

It is not that people don't care about the environment, but people often see the environment as a huge issue affecting the planet, almost too huge, not something they themselves can directly affect.

We need to bring the environmental debate into local communities, and right into people's daily lives.

Not by ignoring the big issues like climate change, but by bringing home to people just how affected they are by the environment on their doorstep.

Being green is about the decisions we take on the things we buy and even how we carry them home.

It is about local planning decisions, taken by local people, in local town halls.

It is about the place we work in – the creation of emissions by the companies we work for, and the products we produce.

And ultimately, it is about our government being willing to take tough decisions at home and convince other governments across the globe to take those tough decisions too.

Challenging behaviour in the home, challenging the behaviour of our businesses, and challenging the behaviour of governments on the international stage.

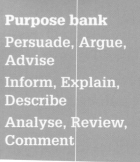

Purpose bank

Persuade, Argue, Advise

Inform, Explain, Describe

Analyse, Review, Comment

1   What is the purpose of this speech? Choose one or more of the words in the 'Purpose bank'.

2   Who do you think might be Charles Kennedy's target audience for this speech?

3   Using the glossary below, try to identify examples of persuasive language in the speech on page 144.

Glossary of rhetorical devices

Alliteration: The repetition of a letter or sound, usually at the start of two or more words in a sentence. Gives a dramatic tone or emphasises a point. *This senseless suffering must stop.*

Direct address: using the pronoun *you* to talk directly to the audience, often to encourage action. *You can make this happen.*

Emotional appeal: an idea intended to create an emotional response, e.g. sympathy. Often refers to children, the elderly, animals. *Imagine how you would feel if this happened to your family.*

Emotive language: a word chosen to create an emotional response in the audience, e.g. sympathy, anger, etc. *Businesses are being forced to make savage cuts.*

First person plural: use of the pronoun *we* to create a feeling of unity between speaker and audience. *None of us can do this alone. We must work together.*

Pattern of three: a list of three words or phrases, sometimes linked by repetition. *This will affect every single one of us: men, women and children.*

Repetition: using a word or phrase more than once to emphasise a point. *We must not give up, we must fight, and fight until we win.*

Rhetorical question: a question that does not expect an answer but leads the audience to the answer which the writer wants. *Should we really be encouraging our children to eat more chips?*

Activity 2

Explore how to deliver a speech.

1   Read Charles Kennedy's speech aloud. Follow the words closely – don't look up from the text.

2   Now try *delivering* the speech: look at your audience as often as possible and try to say the words as if you mean them. What is the difference between reading a speech aloud and delivering it?

Activity 3

Using a speech to get your point of view across can be effective, but you must use all the tools you have. The most effective are your voice and your body. How you control them during a speech can win or lose an argument. Look at the control panel on the right.

1   Choose two or three sentences from the speech on page 144. Write a set of instructions on how to deliver them, using the control panel. For example:

> [**tone**: *concerned*] We [**volume**: *up*] need [**volume**: *down*] to bring the environmental debate into local communities, [**pause**] and [**tone**: *excited* **gesture**: *finger point*] right into people's daily lives.

2   Practise delivering these sentences to a partner. Can your partner suggest ways to make your delivery even more effective?

Delivery control panel

Knowledge about language: **Prepositions**

Prepositions are short words that carry a lot of meaning. They explain the relationship between a noun, adjective or pronoun and the rest of the sentence.

1   Try putting each of the prepositions below into the blank space in the sentence 'He ran _____ the road.' How is the meaning changed?

along   up   down   into   past   near

2   Write the sentence starter 'He worked…' three times. Add a different preposition to each one, then complete the sentences. How do the prepositions change the meaning of the word *worked*?

Peer evaluation

You have been asked to write a speech arguing that schools should teach subjects that are more relevant to students, such as Playing Computer Games, or Fashion Tips.

1   Write up to five sentences that could have come from your speech; include five of the rhetorical devices listed in the glossary on page 145.

2   Deliver your sentences to a partner as effectively as you can, using as many of the features as you can from the control panel above.

3   Which rhetorical devices did you find difficult to write?

4   Which delivery controls did you find difficult to use?

Talking and Listening Activity
Listening

Fabspend – the way forward

Listen to the following speech. You can make notes in any way you like during the speech, though remember that you won't be able to write down every word.

Speech from the leader of the council

1 My fellow councillors, ladies and gentlemen, it is my job this evening to explain to you why the council has decided, after deliberating long and hard, for many months, and listening to the arguments from both sides, *not* to go ahead with either of the original proposals for the area of green space beyond the ring road.

2 It has not been an easy decision and we realise that many of you will be disappointed that the scheme you have supported is not going to go ahead. However, the situation is different now from what it was six months ago, and as the council responsible for ensuring that you continue to have the high-quality local services you deserve, we have had to make some difficult decisions. None of us feels comfortable with this, but we have reached the point where we believe we have no choice – we have no option but to take this course of action – and we do believe that in the end it will yield the best outcome for the largest number of people.

3 Could I remind you, ladies and gentleman, that you returned our party, The Independent Green Liberation party, to power in the council elections only two years ago, with a resounding majority of 2000. That was a big vote of confidence – you have to remember how confident you felt then and trust us now to do the best for you in what are very challenging times.

4 The fact is that when we took over as the leading party, the financial situation in this area was not good. Income in the form of council tax has not been covering our outgoings – we are now under pressure to tighten our belts, draw in our horns and look for ways

to cut our coats according to our cloth. In short, ladies and gentlemen, we are operating this year with a budget deficit of £1,000,000, a situation which cannot be allowed to continue.

5 It was fortuitous, then, if not something of a miracle, when the supermarket chain Fabspend came forward with an offer we couldn't refuse. They have been looking to expand in our area. Yes, I know they already have one store on the west of the town, but they are now looking to build up a customer base on the east side as well. They too have been looking at the green space site – and they see it as an ideal location for their new store. Their market research has revealed that 82 per cent of local residents would welcome a Fabspend store in that location and that it will really be meeting a market need in the area.

6 Fabspend have also offered to provide a play area for young children in their in-store café and, to show their commitment to the environment, to sponsor a tree sapling in the town centre. There is no doubt that Fabspend are very sensitive to the issues around this particular site and mindful of their duty to respect local customs and views. We should remember too, that when the new Fabspend store opens, not only will the retail options of local people be expanded, but there will be employment opportunities too.

7 We will, of course, be taking questions from the floor, but before I open up the discussion, I would like to ask the regional area manager for Fabspend to say a few words to you.

Your task

You can ask the leader of the council to explain any words or phrases that you did not understand; then you should complete the activities below.

1 Give one word, phrase or number in answer to the following questions.
   - How long has the Green Independent Liberation party been in power?
   - How big was its majority?
   - How big is the budget deficit?
   - Who is going to build on the green space?
   - Name one thing that this company is going to do for the local community.

2 In one sentence, sum up the main point of the speech.

3 Give one way the leader of the council tries to show that the council has found it difficult to come to this decision.

4 Explain one way the leader of the council tries to persuade the audience to trust him.

5 Write down three questions you would like to ask the leader of the council.

6 Write down three questions you would like to ask the regional area manager for Fabspend.

7 Does this speech help to persuade you that the council has made the right decision? Give reasons for your answer.

5 Note-taking

You are learning:
- to take notes to summarise information and help your understanding.

You will often need to make notes during your time at school and at work. It is a way of making a lot of information smaller and clearer. It also helps you to pick out and understand the key points of a text you are reading.

Activity 1

Below is an extract from a government website called 'Greener living: a quick guide to what you can do'.

http://www.direct.gov.uk

Save energy and water at home

1 Burning fossil fuels to heat our homes or produce electricity releases carbon emissions, which cause climate change. The energy you use at home is likely to be your biggest contribution to climate change. 80 per cent of it goes on heating and hot water, so this is a good place to look for savings.

2 **Turn down your thermostat**

Turning your thermostat down by one degree could reduce carbon emissions and cut your fuel bills by up to 10 per cent.

3 **Look for the labels**

When buying products that use energy – anything from light bulbs to fridge-freezers – look for the Energy Saving Recommended label or European energy label rating of A or higher. The European energy label also tells you how much water appliances use, so you can choose a more efficient model.

4 **Improve your insulation**

More than half the heat lost in your home escapes through the walls and roof. Cavity wall insulation costs about £260, can take a couple of hours to install, and could save you £160 a year on fuel bills.

When you are researching an argument, you'll need to note points to make your argument and evidence to support them. There are lots of ways of taking notes.

Method A
You can use key words, symbols and abbreviations to make notes. They look like this:

Point: Fossil fuel > heat/electricity = carbon emissions = climate change.
Evidence: 80% energy used in home for heating/hot water.

Method B

Or you can use bullet points or a table. They look like this:

- **Point:** Turn down your thermostat
- **Evidence:** It reduces carbon emissions and cuts fuel bills by 10%

Point	Evidence
Turn down your thermostat	It reduces carbon emissions and cuts fuel bills by 10%

The key points are organised in a list. You can add columns to the table to add information or develop your ideas.

Method C

Or you can use a diagram like this:

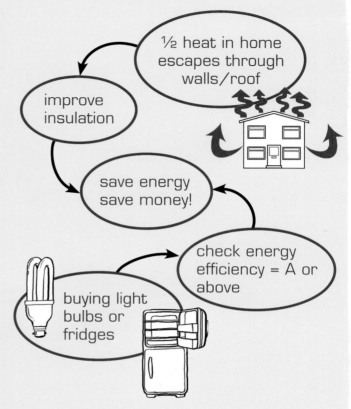

The key points are linked to a central idea and to one another. You can use words and pictures to organise the information. This is more flexible than a list – you can see how all the ideas are connected.

Self-evaluation

1 Use the three different methods to make notes on each of the three paragraphs in this extract from the same website.

2 Which method of note taking do you:
- find easiest?
- think is most effective?

http://www.direct.gov.uk

→Recycle more

Nearly two-thirds of all household rubbish can be recycled. Most councils run doorstep recycling collections for paper, glass and plastics, often more. But local civic amenity sites often accept many other things – from wood and shoes, to textiles and TVs.

→Get composting

Composting food waste reduces climate-change effects. Many local councils offer subsidised compost bins or a home collection for kitchen and garden waste.

→Re-use and repair

Avoiding waste in the first place, by re-using and repairing items, is the most efficient way to reduce waste. For example, buy items that can be re-used rather than disposables, and pass things on when you've finished with them.

6 Organising ideas

You are learning:
- to plan and sequence your ideas for extended writing.

Being a writer is like being an athlete. The more you train and practise, the better you get – and the easier you find it.

Activity 1

First of all, you need to look at the task you have been given, and identify its purpose and target audience. You can then be sure that you are planning a piece of writing that will do what it needs to do – before you write it.

Look at these these two tasks.

> **A** You represent your year group on the school council. Write a speech in which you argue that the school should do more to make itself environmentally friendly.

> **B** Write an article for your school newsletter, arguing that students are already environmentally aware – it's their parents who need to be greener.

1   Identify the purpose and the audience for each task; use the 'Purpose bank' on page 144 to help you. Record your answers in a table like this.

Task	Purpose	Audience
A	Argue	School council
B		

2   For each of these tasks, write a sentence that is appropriate either for the purpose or the intended audience.

3   Think of a new writing task that asks students to argue a case. Make sure your task tells the writer the purpose and audience they are writing for. Swap tasks with a partner. Can your partner identify the purpose and audience?

Activity 2

Once you have identified your purpose and audience, you need to plan the ideas you will use in your writing. Imagine arguing Task A (that your school should become more environmentally friendly).

Think of points that will get your opinion across to the reader and use evidence to prove them. If you were planning Task A, you might have read over this unit so far and come up with these three points and three pieces of evidence.

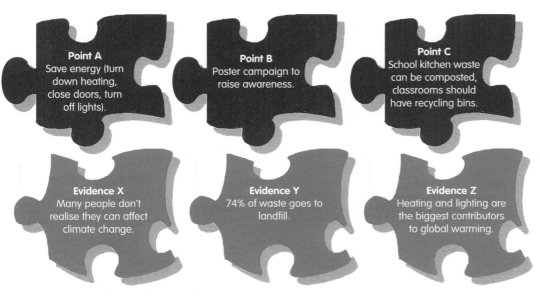

> We should make the school more environmentally friendly.

> Give me three good reasons why we should!

Point A
Save energy (turn down heating, close doors, turn off lights).

Point B
Poster campaign to raise awareness.

Point C
School kitchen waste can be composted, classrooms should have recycling bins.

Evidence X
Many people don't realise they can affect climate change.

Evidence Y
74% of waste goes to landfill.

Evidence Z
Heating and lighting are the biggest contributors to global warming.

1 Which evidence proves which point? Match the points to the evidence.

2 Decide the best order in which to put these points. Write two or three sentences explaining your decision.

3 Re-read Task B and plan the three points and three pieces of evidence you would use. Then sequence your points into the best order.

Knowledge about language: Paragraphs

Paragraphs help readers to understand texts. They divide the story or information into chunks that make their meaning clearer. There are no rules about the length of a paragraph, but there are four reasons to start a new paragraph:

• a change of subject   • a change of time   • a change of place   • a new speaker.

1 Which of the sentences below might you find at the start of a paragraph? Why?

• A hundred years later, in the twentieth century, we began to realise the damage we were doing to our environment.
• It was the first time that scientists understood how this could have happened.
• However, it happened very quickly.
• Another way in which we can prevent global warming is by recycling.
• In America, people were becoming more aware of climate change.
• It was much more difficult than they had imagined.
• 'We can all help,' he replied.

2 You have been asked to write four paragraphs describing your day so far. Write the opening sentence of each paragraph; try to use a different reason for starting each new paragraph.

7 Developing your argument

You are learning:

- to develop your ability to argue a case in writing by including connectives, a counter-argument and rhetorical devices.

Putting forward a successful argument needs more than just good points. You need to organise and express your argument very carefully.

Activity 1

One successful way to win an argument is to guess what your opponent is going to argue – and be ready to tell them why they are wrong.

1   It's bedtime. Write down three points a parent or carer might make to argue that you should go to bed.

2   For each of those three points, make a counter-argument, arguing that you should stay up for another half hour.

3   Look at the plan you made for writing to argue on pages 152–153, Activity 2, question 3.
    a   What point might someone opposing your argument make?
    b   What counter-argument could you make to show that they are wrong?

Activity 2

You have now planned four paragraphs of your article arguing for parents to be more environmentally aware. Three of them will support your argument using evidence; the other one will give a counter-argument and then explain why you think it is wrong.

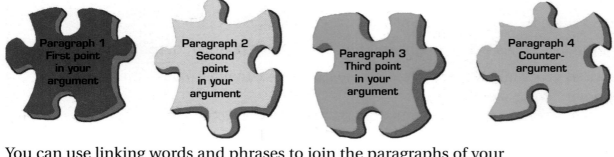

You can use linking words and phrases to join the paragraphs of your article together. Which link could go at the start of each paragraph?

Activity 3

To the right are some sentences from one student's argument that schools should be more environmentally friendly (Task A). Rewrite them to make them more persuasive. Try to include as many rhetorical devices as you can (look at the glossary of rhetorical devices on page 145 to help you).

- Throwing all our rubbish into landfill sites is not very good.
- Having the school's heating up too high is bad.
- Also, people should turn off lights when they don't need them.
- The school is wasting energy and damaging the planet.
- Being environmentally friendly is good.

Knowledge about language: First and third person

Some stories are written in the first person: one of the characters tells the story using the word *I*. Some stories are written in the third person: the narrator uses the words *he*, *she*, *it* and *they* to describe the events of the story.

Writing to argue and persuade may use the first person or the third person. Compare:

> I think that they must do more to help the environment.

> They must do more to help the environment.

1 Which sentence is written in the first person?

2 Which sentence is written in the third person?

3 Which sentence shows that the writer or speaker really means what they say?

4 Which sentence is more powerful and likely to make the reader or listener change their opinion?

5 Which sentence sounds more like a fact than an opinion?

6 Try writing a sentence in the first person and then rewriting it in the third person. Which do you prefer? Why?

Self-evaluation

You have been learning how to plan a piece of writing to argue a case. Now write a set of instructions on how to do this. Remember to include all the different stages you have learned about. You can look back over pages 147–155 to help you.

8 Draft, revise and proofread

You are learning:

● to turn your plan into a successful piece of argumentative (or discursive) writing, by drafting, improving and checking your work.

Once you have done the hard work of planning your writing, you need to make the most of it: by drafting, then improving, then checking it.

Activity 1

Look back at the work you have done planning your article for Task B on page 153. Now you have planned your points and evidence, you can begin writing. You will need to write six paragraphs.

| 1 Introduction | 2 First point | 3 Second point | 4 Third point |

| 5 Counter-argument | 6 Conclusion |

Write a two-sentence introduction to your article, arguing that your parents need to be more environmentally friendly. Your introduction needs to do two things.

- Explain how things are at the moment.
- Explain why you think things should change.

You could begin:

> At the moment ... The problem is ...

Activity 2

When you write your second, third and fourth paragraphs, you should use the points and evidence you have planned. You will need to add an explanation to your point and evidence. The explanation tells your audience how the point and evidence prove your argument.

Point → One way in which our parents could be more environmentally friendly is to try to save energy.

Evidence → Heating and lighting are the two biggest causes of global warming. This suggests that, if our parents turn

Explain → down the heating, remember to close outside doors, and turn off lights when there's nobody in the room, they will be doing a lot to help the environment.

Write a Point–Evidence–Explain paragraph using the point and evidence below.

- Parents can walk to the shops instead of driving their cars.
- Global warming is largely the result of carbon dioxide emissions.

Activity 3

Finally, you need to write your last paragraph: the conclusion. This sums up your opinion and tells the audience what you want them to think and do. A good way to do this is to write a few sentences saying what will happen in the future if:

- what you are suggesting doesn't happen (this will be bad)
- what you are suggesting does happen (this will be good).

Write a two-sentence conclusion to your article. You could begin:

If we do not change ...

However, if we make the changes I am suggesting ...

Activity 4

Now that you have written your first draft, it's time to read it over and improve it. The first thing to do is check your sentences. You should try to use a range of sentences: long and short; simple, compound and complex (see the 'Knowledge about language' box on page 158).

1   Rewrite the paragraph on the right, improving the way sentences are used.

> Another way in which we could improve our school is to make pupils more aware of the problems of global warming and how we need to do more to stop it because a lot of people don't realise that we can do things to help the environment and we could do that by getting pupils in S1 to design posters and we could put them up around the school and maybe have assemblies about it. To get more people interested.

2   You need to check your spelling and punctuation. Writers often make mistakes – but careful checking and correcting are things that make the difference between a piece of writing and a **good** piece of writing. See how many mistakes you can find in the paragraph on the right. Do not correct the mistakes; just make a note of:

   a   How many mistakes did you find on each line?
   b   What are the mistakes?

> i think their is one other thing we should do every first year should be given a flour bed to look after They can grow vegtubles or flowers. growing things make people more aware of the inviroment and nature. it would help us see that we can chang the world and make it a better place to be.

3   If you have done your writing on a computer, then you don't need to check the spelling – the spellchecker has done that for you, right? Wrong! A spellchecker will find no spelling mistakes in this sentence …

   … but it's completely wrong. Why?

> Yew knead two cheque watt ewe right sew ewe our shore their our know missed aches.

Knowledge about language: Simple, compound and complex sentences

1 Simple sentences contain only one verb. In the sentence *The dog chased the cat*, *chased* is the verb.

   Write four simple sentences. Remember to include capital letters and full stops. Underline the verb in each of your sentences.

2 Compound sentences contain two verbs. You can create them by joining two simple sentences using *and* or *but*.

   The dog chased the cat. He did not catch it.
   becomes
   The dog chased the cat but he did not catch it.

   Try to join your simple sentences into two compound sentences using *and* or *but*. Remember to include capital letters and full stops.

3 Complex sentences contain two verbs. They also use linking words (officially known as 'connectives') to join them, such as *because*, *although*, *whenever* or *if* – but they have different rules.
   - One half of a complex sentence does not make sense on its own.
   - You can swap the two halves round without changing the meaning.

   The dog chased the cat. They were enemies.
   becomes
   The dog chased the cat because they were enemies.
   which means the same as
   Because they were enemies, the dog chased the cat.

Try to join your simple sentences into two complex sentences using *because*, *although*, *whenever* or *if*. Remember to include capital letters and full stops. Use the two rules of complex sentences to test whether they really are complex sentences.

Self-evaluation

Below is a list of all the stages of writing you have learned about in this unit.
For each one, write two or three sentences explaining what writers should remember to do to make their planning, drafting, revising and proofreading successful.

Remember:

1 Make notes	2 Plan your paragraphs	3 Write your first draft	4 Improve your writing	5 Check your writing
• •	• • •	• • •	• • •	• •